The New Testament Writer's Worldview

© Bryant C. Buck 2024

All Scripture quotes in this book are from the New American Standard version (NAS) of the Bible unless otherwise noted.

All rights reserved. Without limiting the rights under copyright reserved above, no part of this publication may be reproduced, stored in a retrieval system, or transmitted, in any form or by any means (electronic, mechanical, photocopying, recording or otherwise), without the prior written permission of the copyright owner of this book.

Published by
Lighthouse Christian Publishing
SAN 257-4330
5531 Dufferin Drive
Savage, Minnesota, 55378
United States of America

www.lighthousechristianpublishing.com

TABLE OF CONTENTS

INTRODUCTION..1

CHAPTER 1 – THE NEW TESTAMENT WRITERS ALL JEWISH IN THEIR WORLDVIEW...............5

CHAPTER 2 – THE FAITH ONCE DELIVERED...9

CHAPTER 3 – TIME PERCEPTION OF THE NEW TESTAMENT WRITERS................................13

CHAPTER 4 – THE TEMPLE AND THE SYNAGOGUE...19

CHAPTER 5 – JEWS, PROSLEYTES, AND GOD-FEARERS...26

CHAPTER 6 – HOW NEW TESTAMENT WRITERS VIEWED THE SCRIPTURES...........................32

CHAPTER 7 – HOW NEW TESTAMENT WRITERS VIEWED THE COMMANDMENTS...................38

CHAPTER 8 – HOW NEW TESTAMENT WRITERS VIEWED THE ORDINANCES.........................43

CHAPTER 9 – THE JERUSALEM COUNCIL......49

CHAPTER 10 – THE NEW TESTAMENT WRITERS' OVERALL VIEW OF THE LAW.......................54

The New Testament Writer's Worldview

Bryant C. Buck

The New Testament Writer's Worldview

CHAPTER 11 – TWO VERSES OF PARTICULAR INTEREST..59

CHAPTER 12 – THE NEW TESTAMENT WRITERS AND THE SABBATH – PART 1.........................63

CHAPTER 13 – THE NEW TESTAMENT WRITERS AND THE SABBATH – PART 2.........................71

CHAPTER 14 – TWO OTHER DIFFERENCES OF NOTE...76

CHAPTER 15 – JEWS, GENTILES, AND THE CHURCH..83

CHAPTER 16 – WHAT THE NEW TESTAMENT WRITERS EMPHASIZED – PART 1....................89

CHAPTER 17 – WHAT THE NEW TESTAMENT WRITERS EMPHASIZED – PART 2....................93

CHAPTER 18 - HOUSE CHURCHES IN THE NEW TESTAMENT...99

CHAPTER 19 – WHICH COMMANDMENTS DID THE NEW TESTAMENT WRITERS KEEP?....................107

CHAPTER 20 – PUTTING IT ALL TOGETHER....114

CHAPTER 21 – WHERE DO WE GO FROM HERE? 120

POSTSCRIPT..126

BIBLIOGRAPHY..132

INTRODUCTION

This book is an effort to bring out how the New Testament writers viewed Christianity and the world. We understand how they viewed Christianity and the world through their writings in the New Testament. Did they view everything the same as Christians do today? No, they did not. Did they view many things the same as Christians do today? Yes, they viewed many things the same as we do today. This book will not focus on those things that they saw the same as we do, but rather on those things that they saw differently.

First, let me define Christianity as used in this book. Christianity is the religion of Jesus Christ the Son of God and the Savior of the world. To be a Biblical Christian, a person must repent of his sins and accept Jesus Christ as his Lord and Savior. The Bible calls this experience getting saved and being born again. This salvation experience is only accomplished through grace by faith without any works of the law.

Now I believe that the writers of the New Testament had the same view on salvation as do Bible-believing Christians today. They believed that Jesus Christ is the Son of God and the Savior of the world. They believed that an individual had to repent of his sins and accept Jesus Christ as his Lord and Savior in order to be saved. Moreover, the New Testament writers believed that this salvation experience was only accomplished through grace by faith without any works of the law. Since the New Testament writers and modern Bible-believing Christians agree on these basics of the Chrisitan faith, these beliefs will be discussed only briefly in the latter part of this book.

Similarly, the New Testament writers believed in water baptism by immersion after a person accepted Jesus Christ as his Lord and Savior. The vast majority of Bible-believing Christians believe the same about water baptism today. Likewise, the New Testament writers believed that the Bible is the inspired Word of God. Bible-believing Christians believe the same today. Moreover, the New Testament writers believed that Christians should turn away from sin and lead a life of righteousness dedicated to God. Again, Bible-believing Christians believe the same today. So these beliefs will be discussed only briefly in the latter part of this book.

The major difference between Evangelicals and Fundamentalists on the one hand and Charismatics and Pentecostals on the other hand is their belief about the baptism in the Holy Spirit. Evangelicals and Fundamentalists believe that a Christian is baptized in the Holy Spirit when he repents and accepts Jesus Christ as his Lord and Savior. Charismatics and Pentecostals, however, believe that a Christian is baptized in the Holy Spirit after his salvation experience. To put this another way, Charismatics and Pentecostals believe that there are two distinct experiences in the Holy Spirit while Evangelicals and Fundamentalists believe that there is only one distinct experience in the Holy Spirit. Plus, Charismatics and Pentecostals believe in speaking in tongues today while most Evangelicals and Fundamentalists do not. As far as I can see in the Bible, Christians in the 1st Century church had two distinct experiences in the Holy Spirit. Plus, there is more than one occasion recorded where they spoke in tongues. So I am with the Charismatics and the Pentecostals on this issue. All this being said, the baptism in the Holy Spirit will only be discussed briefly near the end of this book.

What this book endeavors to do is examine where the writers of the New Testament had a different worldview than do Bible-believing Christians today. We will use the actual events recorded in Acts and the New Testament writers' own words recorded in the epistles to bring out where their worldview differed from ours today. We will also use the gospels along with Acts and the epistles to show their view of the Old Testament. The surprise will be how many events recorded in Acts and statements the New Testament writers made in the epistles are almost universally overlooked by modern Bible-believing Christians. But the events and the statements are right there in front of us. We just read right by them or have been trained to overlook them.

Since all Bible-believing Christian agree on certain basics of the faith, why don't they agree on all matters of faith and doctrine? They disagree because they interpret various parts of the Bible differently. Is this book an effort to resolve all those differences of interpretation? Absolutely not. This book is an effort to examine how the writers of the New Testament saw the world and the Scriptures. As noted above, on many basic beliefs they saw the Scriptures the same as we do today. But in certain areas they did not see the Scriptures at all like we do today.

This book deals primarily with the worldview of the New Testament writers in the areas where they differ from modern Bible-believing Christians. The 1st Century New Testament writers had a definite worldview, and I will attempt to bring out their worldview in this book. Moreover, the 1st Century writers knew that they had received "the faith which was once delivered unto the saints." (Jude 3 KJV) They also foresaw that even believers themselves would depart from this original faith. In fact, the apostle Paul gave the church this warning: "For I know this, that after my departing shall grievous wolves enter in among you, not sparing the flock. Also of your own selves shall men arise, speaking perverse things, to draw away disciples after them." (Acts 20:29-30 KJV) We do not want any of the beliefs of those who departed the faith. We want the original faith of the 1st Century New Testament writers – "the faith which was once delivered unto the saints."

CHAPTER 1

THE NEW TESTAMENT WRITERS ALL JEWISH IN THEIR WORLDVIEW

The first thing that we want to note in our consideration of how to interpret the Scriptures is that the men whom the Lord inspired to write the New Testament were all Jewish in their worldview. In fact, with the exception of Luke, they were all born Jews. Concerning Luke, the historians disagree. Some believe that he was a Hellenistic Jew (a proselyte to Judaism) before he became a Christian. Others believe that he converted to Christianity under the ministry of the apostle Paul. Either way, under the influence of the Jewish Christians whom he joined, Luke took on the Jewish worldview of 1st Century Christianity. Since all the other New Testament writers were Jews by birth, they all had a Jewish worldview. Now the Jewish worldview has changed somewhat since the 1st Century A.D.; so specifically we want to understand the worldview of 1st Century Jews. Moreover, since the revelation of the New Testament was given to men with a Jewish worldview who accepted Jesus Christ as their Lord and Savior, we want the worldview of those born-again Jews.

Did finding Jesus Christ as their Lord and Savior change the worldview of those 1st Century Jews? Definitely yes. However, their worldview did not change as much as many of us would like to believe today. For example, the Jews understood time differently than the Romans did. In our world today we follow the observation of time passed unto us by the Romans.

The New Testament Writer's Worldview

However, the Jews did not observe time as the Romans did. They understood the day, the week, the month, and the year all differently than the Romans did. Only in the week did the Jewish understanding of time come close to coinciding with the Roman understanding of time. Nevertheless, even with the week, the Jewish understanding was not exactly the same as the Roman understanding. In this book, I devote a whole chapter to the 1st Century Jewish understanding of time.

From the letters of Paul, we know that the traditional Jewish view of the law changed with 1st Century Jewish believers. However, their view of the law did not change as much as many modern Christians believe it did. This would be particularly true in regard to Old Testament commandments. Although the 1st Century Jewish apostles clearly saw that believers could not become righteous by the law or stay righteous by the law, they still viewed Old Testament commandments as dictates to be obeyed. Part of our problem here is that most Christians today don't understand the divisions of the law perceived by 1st Century Jewish believers. The law didn't include just commandments, but also statutes, judgments, and ordinances. I will take more than one chapter to delve into the understanding of the law as viewed by 1st Century Jewish Christians. From what I can see in the New Testament, the early Jewish Christians believed that some parts of the law were fulfilled by Jesus Christ, but that other parts were not.

Paul wrote these words concerning the revelation given to the Jews: "For I could wish that I myself were accursed, separated from Christ for the sake of my brethren, my kinsmen according to the flesh, who are Israelites, to whom belongs the adoption as sons, and the glory and covenants and the giving of the Law and the temple service and the promises, whose are the fathers, and from whom is the Christ according to the flesh, who is over all, God blessed forever. Amen." (Romans 9:3-5) When you were saved, God adopted you as one of his sons or daughters. Where did that come from? The Jews (Israelites). We are living in the promises of God today. Where did they come from? The Jews (Israelites). We, Gentile believers, need to face this simple truth: If 1st Century Jewish Christians had not received the revelation of "the adoption as sons" and "the promises," we would still be lost in our sins today. We certainly owe much to those Jewish apostles who received the revelation by which we are now saved.

Where did the 1st Century Jewish believers go to church? There is no evidence that they had their own church buildings as we do today. But there is plenty of evidence that those early believers went to the temple in Jerusalem and to synagogues outside Jerusalem. In fact, they did so until they were put out of Judaism around 70 A.D. Why did the 1st Century Jewish Christians continue to go to the temple and to synagogues? We will take a full chapter to explore the behavior of the 1st Century Jewish believers in this regard.

Finally, most Christians today do not know that the Jewish synagogues in the diaspora (the nations outside of Israel) had three distinct groups of people. First, there were Jews who were born Jews. Second, there were converts to Judaism. The converts not only accepted the moral teachings of Judaism, but they also accepted circumcision. Because the converts accepted Judaism, they were viewed as full Jews by those who were Jews by birth. Third, there were God-fearers. These people accepted the moral teachings of Judaism, but not circumcision. Because they did not get circumcised, they were still viewed as Gentiles by the other Jews in the synagogue. We will take a full chapter to look at these different groups in the Jewish synagogue and how this should affect our understanding of Acts in particular and the New Testament epistles in general.

So I repeat this very simple point: All the writers of the New Testament were Jewish in their worldview. Yes, they accepted Jesus Christ as their Lord and Savior. They understood the things in the Old Testament which Jesus fulfilled through His death on the cross. Nevertheless, they still maintained a Jewish worldview, having great respect for the Old Testament in general and the Ten Commandments in particular. In fact, their worldview was an essential part of "the faith which was once delivered unto the saints." (Jude 3)

CHAPTER 2

THE FAITH ONCE DELIVERED

"Beloved, when I gave all diligence to write unto you of the common salvation, it was needful for me to write unto you, and exhort you that ye should earnestly contend for the faith which was once delivered unto the saints." (Jude 3 KJV) The New American Standard renders this same verse: "Beloved, while I was making every effort to write you about our common salvation, I felt the necessity to write to you appealing that you contend earnestly for the faith which was once for all handed down to the saints." The faith "once delivered" to the saints is the faith "once for all handed down" to the saints. The key word in both translations is "once." The Christian faith was once delivered to the saints through the original apostles of Jesus Christ. Therefore, the truths of the Christian faith don't need to be delivered to the saints again unless those truths have been corrupted by succeeding generations.

Since Jude was one of the last of the New Testament writers, "the faith which was once for all handed down to the saints" was handed down to them before Jude wrote his letter. In other words, the faith once delivered to the saints was delivered to them before the New Testament was completed. Since the last book included in the New Testament was written before 95 A.D., then the faith once delivered to the saints was delivered before 95 A.D.

What does Jude's statement concerning the faith once delivered mean for us? If the Christian faith has remained the same since 95 A.D., then we still have the faith once delivered today. However, if succeeding generations after 95 A.D. corrupted the original faith once delivered, then we only have those parts of the faith which succeeding generations did not corrupt. If the Holy Spirit led us out of some of those corruptions and back to the truth, then we have returned to the original faith to the degree that we have allowed the Holy Spirit to lead us back to the truth. The historical truth is that during the 2nd and 3rd Centuries A.D. many Christians gradually turned away from certain aspects of the faith originally handed down to the saints. Then in the 4th and 5th Centuries A.D. this turning away from the truth became a massive departure in which the vast majority of Christians turned away from the original Christian faith. The problem for sincere Christians ever since has been to find their way back to the faith "once for all handed down" to the saints.

Consider the following Scripture. "Therefore repent and return, so that your sins may be wiped away, in order that times of refreshing may come from the presence of the Lord; and that He may send Jesus, the Christ appointed for you, whom heaven must receive until the period of restoration of all things about which God spoke by the mouth of His holy prophets from ancient time." (Acts 3:19-21) Notice that this Scripture states that Jesus must be received in heaven "until the period of restoration of all things." Jesus is still in heaven; He has yet to return to earth. Therefore, the period of restoration of all things must not be complete. In consequence, there must be truths that were part of the faith originally delivered to the saints that still need to be restored to the church.

Ask yourself this question: Do I want the faith originally delivered to the saints even if it means giving up traditions which cannot be supported by the Scriptures? Furthermore, do I take the Scriptures at face value when they align with what my church teaches, but dismiss the Scriptures when they don't? Understanding the Jewish worldview of the original apostles should help us determine how much of the faith that we have today is the same as the faith "once delivered" to the early Christian church.

CHAPTER 3

TIME PERCEPTION OF THE NEW TESTAMENT WRITERS

We are so ingrained in the way which we think about time that it is hard for us to realize that people did not always think about time the way we do. We think in Roman time. In Roman time a day starts at midnight and ends at the following midnight. A week begins at midnight at the start of Sunday and ends at midnight seven days later at the end of Saturday going into another Sunday. In Roman time months are either 30 or 31 days long (with the exception of February) and start without relation to the moon. Finally, in Roman time the year starts on the 1st of January during the winter and ends on December 31st twelve months later. The Roman year is 365 days long with the exception that every fourth year it is 366 days long.

Did the writers of the New Testament perceive time the way the Romans did? No, they did not. The writers of the New Testament understood time the way that time is laid out in the Bible. We shall take this chapter to understand how the New Testament writers perceived time. Moreover, we shall take this chapter to comprehend how God laid out time in the Bible.

"God called the light day, and the darkness He called night. And there was evening, and there was morning, one day." (Genesis 1:5) "And God called the expanse heaven. And there was evening and there was morning, a second day." (Genesis 1:8) Likewise, in Genesis 1:13, 19, 23, and 31 God defines a day as evening and morning. In the Bible a day starts at sundown before evening and ends just before sundown the following evening. God never gives another definition of a day anywhere else in the Bible.

In Roman time, then, God's day starts on the average at 6 PM and ends on the average at 6 PM the following evening. So God's day starts on the average six hours before the Roman day begins. God repeats His definition of a day six times in Genesis chapter 1. He never changes His definition of a day anywhere else in the Bible. In consequence, when we think of any day in the Bible, we need to think in terms of a twenty-four-period beginning at sundown and ending just before the following sundown.

The Roman week starts at 12 midnight on Sunday and ends seven days later at 12 midnight at the end of Saturday going into the following Sunday. God's week is also seven days long, but it starts at sundown on one Saturday evening and ends seven days later just before sundown on the following Saturday evening. So God's week starts on average 6 hours before the Roman week begins. God's week and the Roman week both have seven days, but they are not exactly the same because God's week aligns with God's day (which stats at sundown) while the Roman week aligns with the Roman day (which starts at midnight).

"'And it shall be from new moon to new moon and from sabbath to sabbath, all mankind will come to bow down before Me,' says the LORD." (Isaiah 66:23) God's month starts with the new moon. In other words, God's month starts the day the first sliver of a new moon appears after the last sliver of the previous moon disappears. God measures months "from new moon to new moon." God never changes the definition of a month anywhere else in the Bible. A month is always from one new moon to the next new moon.

The time period from one new moon to the next new moon is 29 and ½ days. This is one full day shorter than the average Roman month of 30 and ½ days. The Roman month is an artificial invention of man. It is tied neither to the sun nor the moon. "Then God said, 'Let there be lights in the expanse of the heavens to separate the day from the night, and let them be for signs and for seasons and for days and years.'" (Genesis 1:14) Biblically the day is defined by the sun in its relation to the earth while the month is defined by the moon in its relation to the earth. God defines days, weeks, months, and years by the lights in the sky. The Roman definition of days, weeks, months, and years is artificial and does not follow the lights that God put in the sky.

"Now the LORD said to Moses and Aaron in the land of Egypt, 'This month shall be the beginning of months for you; it is to be the first month of the year to you.'" (Exodus 12:1-2) The historical records tell us that God spoke this word to Moses in the springtime of the year on the Roman calendar. The historical time during which the Jews have kept Passover bears this out. God declared that Passover was to be observed on the fourteenth day of the first month. (See Exodus 12:6 and Leviticus 23:5.) The Jews have always observed Passover in the spring. In fact, the Jews have always observed Passover between late March and late April. So the first month of God's year is in the spring.

Now God's year is different from the Roman year in that it follows both the moon and the sun. The Roman year follows the sun, but not the moon. When the Romans figured out that it takes 365 and ¼ days for the earth to orbit the sun, they set their year to 365 days for three years and 366 days in leap year. But God's year doesn't work this way. In God's calendar months go back and forth between 29 day months and 30 day months So in twelve Biblical months there are 354 days – 11 and ¼ days short of the time necessary for the earth to make one complete orbit around the sun. How did the Jews compensate for this shortfall of days to keep the year beginning in the spring?

The Jews watched the sky to set the first month of their year as close to the spring equinox as possible. However, they always started their year so that Passover would occur after the spring equinox. On the Roman calendar, this meant that the Jews always started their year between roughly March 8th and April 9th. Over a period of nineteen years, this would result in 12 years of 12 months and 7 years of 13 months. So twelve of the nineteen years would have 354 days and seven of the nineteen years would have either 383 or 384 days. But at the end of nineteen years, the new moon starting the year would be at the same time in relation to the sun as it was nineteen years earlier.

In Roman time we think of years as periods of equal number of days. Yet even in Roman time the number of days in leap year is not equal to the number of days in each of the three previous years. God, however, does not think of years in terms of equal number of days or even equal number of months. God sets the year by the spring equinox and then uses new moon months to fill out the Biblical year. Since we are so ingrained with Roman time, it is difficult for us to think in God's time, particularly when it comes to God's year.

Now why is all this so important? In Daniel chapter 2 God through his prophet Daniel predicted in succession four kingdoms that would rule the known world. The fourth of those kingdoms was the Roman Empire. The same four kingdoms were predicted again in Daniel chapter 7. In Daniel 7:23 we read, 'Thus he said: 'The fourth beast will be a fourth kingdom on the earth, which will be different from all other kingdoms and will devour the whole earth and tread it down and crush it.'" The "fourth kingdom on the earth" was Rome.

In Daniel 7:25 Daniel's prophecy continues: "He will speak out against the Most High and wear down the saints of the Highest One, and he will intend to make alterations in time and in law; and they will be given into his hand for a time, times, and half a time." The "beast king" who will rule the end-time successor state to the Roman Empire will "MAKE ALTERATIONS IN TIME AND LAW." The Romans have already made the alterations with time. The Romans have altered the day, the week, the month, and the year. The Roman system of keeping time has taken away from our understanding of God's system of keeping time. But God has never changed how He keeps time. Moreover, all the Bible writers operated in God's system of time – not in the Roman system of time.

How did the Biblical perception of time influence the thinking of the New Testament writers? I will give two examples. "Leave out the court which is outside the temple and do not measure It, for it has been given to the nations; and they will tread under foot the holy city for forty-two months." (Revelation 11:2) From this Scripture and others, Bible scholars have generally interpreted the time period of the Great Tribulation as forty-two months.

They further go on to interpret this time period as three and one-half years. However, they are thinking three and one-half Roman years, and that is incorrect. Since God's new moon months are shorter than artificial Roman months, the Great Tribulation is shorter than three and one-half Roman years. When interpreting the New Testament writers, we need to think in terms of Biblical months.

The second example involves the Biblical day. "On the first day of the week, when we gathered together to break bread, Paul began talking to them, intending to leave the next day, and he prolonged his message until midnight." (Acts 20:7) When we read a verse that states "the first day of the week," we tend to think Sunday. But as we have already noted, the first day of God's week does not equate to Sunday. The first day of God's week starts on the average six hours before the Roman Sunday begins and ends on the average six hours before the Roman Sunday concludes. A Biblical event on the first day of the week could have occurred on Sunday, but it could also have occurred on Saturday evening. That's why we need to think in terms of the Biblical day – not in terms of the Roman day.

Did the meeting recorded in Acts 20:7 happen on Sunday or on Saturday evening? The verse concludes: "And he prolonged his message until midnight." For Paul to keep preaching until midnight on the first day of the week, this meeting had to occur on Saturday evening. Daytime meetings do not last until midnight; evening meetings occasionally last until midnight. The meeting recorded in Acts 20:7 did not take place on a Roman Sunday as most modern Christians believe. The meeting in Acts 20:7 occurred on a Saturday evening. The New

Testament writers would not have read this any other way.

Finally, I will give an example of a Biblical impossibility for a holiday celebrated by most Christians today. Most Christians celebrate December 25th as the birthday of Jesus Christ. But December 25th is a Roman calendar date. As noted earlier in this chapter none of the writers of the New Testament kept track of time by the Roman calendar. They all kept track of time by the Biblical calendar. If Jesus was born in December on the Roman calendar, then the New Testament writers would have said that He was born in the tenth month (on the Biblical calendar). If He was born on the 15th day of the tenth month, then they would have said that He was born on the 15th day of the tenth month. If that date had coincided with the 25th day of December in the year that Jesus was born, then it would not have coincided with the 25th day of December in most years after He was born. For example, maybe the next year the 15th day of the tenth month would have been on the 17th day of December and the following year it would have been on the 27th day of December. A Roman calendar date for the birth of Jesus Christ is a Biblical impossibility.

In closing this chapter I will add that no Bible scholar believes that Jesus Christ was born in December. A minority of Bible scholars believe that Jesus was born in the Spring while the majority of them believe that He was born in the Fall. Why they believe this is beyond the scope of this book. Let us just note that there is no Biblical record of any 1st Century Christian observing Christmas or even the birth of Jesus Christ.

CHAPTER 4

THE TEMPLE AND THE SYNAGOGUE

Where did the New Testament writers assemble for meetings? Most modern Christians believe that the New Testament writers went to church the same as we do today. The truth is that they never went to church. Why? There were no church buildings for separate meetings for Christians in the 1st Century A.D. When the New Testament writers assembled for meetings, they either went to the temple, the synagogue, or somebody's house.

Let's start by considering the structure of 1st Century Judaism. The center of Jewish worship at that time was the temple. The temple was in Jerusalem, but there was only one temple. So where did the Jews in Israel worship if they lived too far to go to the temple? And where did the Jews who were scattered among the nations worship? Most of them lived hundreds of miles from the temple. So going to the temple every Sabbath was not an option for the Jews in the diaspora (those who were scattered outside of Israel). Where the Jews who lived too far to go to the temple assembled was in synagogues. Quite simply, synagogues were the buildings where Jews who lived too far to go to the temple assembled for worship every Sabbath.

Now when Jesus commissioned His disciples to go to the nations (Matthew 28:18-20), He didn't tell them to stop going to the temple or the synagogue. This comes as a surprise to many modern Christians because they are accustomed to meeting every week in a church building.

But there were no church buildings in the 1st Century A.D. So meeting in a church building was not an option for 1st Century Christians. Where did these early Christians meet after Jesus ascended to heaven?

In Acts 3:1 we read: "Now Peter and John were going up the temple at the ninth hour, the hour of prayer." If Judaism was done away with when Jesus ascended to heaven, why were Peter and John still going to the temple? First, Jesus never told them to stop going to the temple. Second, Peter and John and the other early believers in Jerusalem still thought of themselves as Jews. From their perspective, Jesus had come to fulfill the predictions of the prophets. In effect, then, Jesus had come to perfect a Judaism that had gotten off track.

Consider the words of Jesus to the Samaritan woman at the well: "You worship what you do not know; we worship what we know, for salvation is from the Jews." (John 4:22) When Jesus said, "We worship what we know," He was clearly identifying as a Jew. In fact, His next statement reinforced that identification: "Salvation is from the Jews." Moreover, Jesus as a Jew died for our salvation. Without Jesus' death on the cross, there is no salvation. So in His own person Jesus made His statement true: "Salvation is from the Jews." That's what all the New Testament writers believed – that salvation was from the Jews just as Jesus declared.

Was the Acts 3 visit of Peter and John to the temple an isolated incident? The answer is no. In the previous chapter of Acts we read this verse: "Day by day continuing with one accord in the temple, and breaking bread from house to house, they were taking their meals together with gladness and sincerity of heart." (Acts 2:46) "Day by day" the members of the early church went to "the temple." So they went to the temple on a regular basis. This verse also records that these early believers met "from house to house." But they did not meet in separate church buildings. The early church in Jerusalem that grew like a wildfire met in the temple and from house to house.

Until Acts chapter 8, the early Christians assembled in the temple and from house to house. But after the death of Stephen, we read these words: "And on that day a great persecution began against the church in Jerusalem, and they were all scattered throughout the regions of Judea and Samaria, except the apostles." (Acts 8:1b) From this time on very few Christians assembled in the temple in Jerusalem. Where did they meet at that time? "But Saul began ravaging the church, entering house after house, and dragging off men and women, he would put them in prison." (Acts 8:3) The church in this verse refers to the early believers who believed in Jesus Christ. This verse also tells us where these early believers met – in "house after house." When the 1st Century Christians in Judea and Samaria could not meet in the temple, they met in houses.

In Acts 11 we find the first mention in the New Testament of a church outside of Jerusalem –the church at Antioch. Here again the church refers to the believers who assembled together – not to the building in which they assembled. For example, in Acts 11:26b we read: "And for an entire year they (Barnabas and Saul) met with the church and taught considerable numbers; and the disciples were first called Christians in Antioch." Here the church clearly refers to the believers who were meeting together. Here we also find these early believers "first called Christians." But although they were called Christians at

Antioch, we find no record here that the name by which others called them changed their perception of who they were in Christ.

In Acts 13 Paul and Barnabas were sent out by the church at Antioch to go to the Gentiles. If Paul and Barnabas were to change their self-identification because of their mission to the Gentiles, this should clearly come out in the record of their trip. First, they went to Cyprus and then they went to Asia Minor. In Acts 13:14 we read: "But going on from Perga, they arrived in Pisidian Antioch, and on the Sabbath day they went into the synagogue and sat down." Why did Paul and Barnabas do this? They had been sent out on a mission to the Gentiles, yet they went right into a synagogue of the Jews. We will leave the answer to this question for the next chapter. Suffice it to say at this point that Paul and Barnabas still identified as Jews or they would not have gone into a Jewish synagogue in Pisidian Antioch.

After Paul preached Christ to those assembled at the synagogue in Pisidian Antioch, we read these words: "Now when the meeting of the synagogue had broken up, many of the Jews and of the God-fearing proselytes followed Paul and Barnabas, who, speaking to them, were urging them to continue in the grace of God." (Acts 13:43) We will return to this verse in the next chapter to talk about who "the God-fearing proselytes" were. At this point we will just note that Paul and Barnabas didn't tell anyone to get out of the synagogue or join the church. They just urged those who responded to Paul's message "to continue in the grace of God."

From Pisidian Antioch Paul and Barnabas went to Iconium. "In Iconium they entered the synagogue of the Jews together, and spoke in such a manner that a large number of people believed, both of Jews and Gentiles." (Acts 14:1) The point here is that Paul and Barnabas took the same approach in Iconium as they did in Pisidian Antioch: the first place they went was the synagogue of the Jews. Their missionary trip continued with stops in Lystra and Derbe. Did they go into the synagogues in those cities? The Bible does not mention whether or not they did. However, since we see that they had already established the pattern of going to the local synagogues in Pisidian Antioch and Iconium, it is reasonable to believe that they did the same in Lystra and Derbe.

When Paul and Silas went on the second mission to the Gentiles, we finally find recorded where they did not go into the synagogue to start their outreach. When they arrived in Philippi, we read: "And on the Sabbath day we went outside the gate to a riverside, where we were supposing there would be a place of prayer; and we sat down and began speaking to the women who had assembled." (Acts 16:13) Why did they do this? Although I cannot prove this to you, I believe that they went to where they believed there was a place of prayer on the Sabbath because there was no synagogue in Philippi. The Bible records that the meeting at the riverside occurred on the Sabbath. If there had been a synagogue in Philippi, wouldn't Paul and Silas have gone there instead?

What Paul and Barnabas did at the next place they stopped reinforces the probability that there was no synagogue in Philippi. "Now when they had traveled through Amphipolis and Apolonia, they came to Thessalonica, where there was a synagogue of the Jews." (Acts 17:1) What did Paul do? "And according to Paul's custom, he went to them, and for three Sabbaths reasoned with them from the Scriptures." (Acts 17:2) This verse tells me that it was Pauls' custom to go to the synagogue. (It also tells me that it was his custom to observe the Sabbath.) Throughout his missionary journeys Paul maintained the custom of going to the Jewish synagogue first whenever he arrived in a new city. The evidence is clear: Even as a believer in Jesus Christ, Paul still thought of himself as a Jew. So he continued to go the synagogue every place he went (if there was a synagogue there).

What I have brought out in this chapter will no doubt come as a shock to many Christians today. The New Testament writers all went to the temple as long as they could. And from the evidence of Pauls' missionary journeys, it appears that they all went to the synagogue as long as they could. Not until the early Jewish believers in Christ were put out of the synagogue did their visits to the synagogue come to an end. The official Jewish excommunication of Jewish Christians from the synagogue took place in 70 A.D. We need to realize that all the writers of the New Testament were maintaining contact with Judaism until that date.

In closing this chapter, I will comment briefly on the synagogue service in the 1st Century. Although there have been some changes in the synagogue service over the centuries, two elements have remained constant – the reading of the law and the reading of the prophets. So every 1st Century synagogue service included both a reading from the law and a reading from the prophets. For Jews then as today, the law was the first five books of the Bible. Thus every 1st Century synagogue service included a reading from the Torah – that is, the first five books of the Bible.

Interestingly, we have recorded where Jesus gave the reading from the prophets in the synagogue. "And He came to Nazareth, where He had been brought up; and as was His custom, He entered the synagogue on the Sabbath, and stood up to read. And the book of the prophet Isaiah was handed to Him. And He opened the book and found the place where it was written, 'THE SPIRIT OF THE LORD IS UPON ME, BECAUSE HE ANOINTED ME TO PREACH THE GOSPEL TO THE POOR. HE HAS SENT ME TO PROCLAIM RELEASE TO THE CAPTIVES, AND RECOVERY OF SIGHT TO THE BLIND, TO SET FREE THOSE WHO ARE OPPRESSED, TO PROCLAIM THE FAVORABLE YEAR OF THE LORD.'" (Luke 4:16-19) Of course, Jesus selected this Scripture because He was fulfilling it in Himself. "And he began to say to them, 'Today this Scripture has been fulfilled in your hearing.'" (Luke 4:21) From where was Jesus reading in Isaiah? Jesus was reading from Isaiah 61:1-2. But in line with what we have considered in this chapter, Jesus was giving the reading of the prophets in the synagogue.

CHAPTER 5

JEWS, PROSELYTES, AND GOD-FEARERS

Most Christians today don't know much about the Jewish synagogue of the 1st century A.D. Yet we have already noted that the Jewish Christian writers of the New Testament regularly went to the synagogue. Moreover, we have also noted that the Jewish believers in the 1st Century Christian church regularly went to the synagogue. Much of the Christian church today believes that all things Jewish were done away with the day that Christ ascended to heaven. However, the historical record from the New Testament itself does not bear this out.

The Jewish synagogue of the 1st Century basically consisted of three categories of people – Jews, proselytes, and God-fearers. The Jews were people who were born Jews. In other words, their natural parents were Jews; so these people were Jews by birth. The proselytes were former Gentiles who made a full conversion to Judaism. They accepted not only the moral teachings of Judaism, but also physical circumcision. The God-fearers were Gentiles who attended the synagogue services, but did not make a full conversion to Judaism. They accepted the moral teachings of Judaism, but did not accept physical circumcision.

Now the Jews themselves regarded the proselytes as full Jews. Once these former Gentiles accepted circumcision, they were no longer regarded as Gentiles. The proselytes were considered Jews the same as those who were born Jews. But this was not true of the God-fearers. Although they accepted the moral teachings of Judaism, they were still considered Gentiles by the other members of the synagogue because they refused circumcision. From the few historical records that we have on 1st Century Judaism, most synagogues in the diaspora contained all three categories of people.

In Acts 6:1 (KJV) we read the following Scripture regarding the church in Jerusalem: "And in those days, when the number of the disciples was multiplied, there arose a murmuring of the Grecians against the Hebrews, because their widows were neglected in the daily ministration." Who were the Grecians referred to in this verse? Since the gospel had not yet gone to the Gentiles, they couldn't be Gentiles. The New American Standard version of Acts 6:1 is very helpful here: "Now at this time while the disciples were increasing, a complaint arose on the part of the Hellenistic Jews against the native Hebrews, because their widows were being overlooked in the daily serving of food." The Grecians were Hellenistic Jews. In other words, they spoke Greek and adopted many Greek customs. Nevertheless, they were considered Jews because they accepted circumcision. Were they all proselytes to Judaism? The passage in Acts 6 does not tell us whether they were proselytes or not. As Greek culture had been predominant in Palestine for almost 300 years at that time, it is likely that some of these Hellenistic Jews were born Jews and that some of them were proselytes. The point is that from early on the Christian church didn't just consist of natural-born Jews who accepted Jesus Christ. It also included Jewish proselytes who believed in Jesus Christ.

The New Testament Writer's Worldview

When Paul and Barnabas went on the first missionary trip to the Gentiles, the relationship between the 1st Century church and the synagogue comes into clearer view. "But going on from Perga, they arrived at Pisidian Antioch, and on the Sabbath day they went into the synagogue and sat down." (Acts 13:14) When Paul and Barnabas arrived in Pisidian Antioch, where did they go? They went to the Jewish synagogue. Some modern Christians have argued that they did this to reach out to the Jews first. But the first words of Paul's message paint a different picture. "Paul stood up, and motioning with his hand said, 'Men of Israel, and you who fear God, listen.'" (Acts 13:16) Paul started his message by addressing both the Jews ("men of Israel") and the God-fearers ("you who fear God"). Since the "men of Israel" were the Jews, "you who fear God" were the God-fearing Gentiles. Yes, the gospel was "to the Jew first and also to the Greek." (Romans 1:16) But when Paul had the opportunity, Paul took the gospel message to both groups at the same time. He clearly did so at Pisidian Antioch.

When Paul finished his message to Jews and God-fearers in the synagogue at Pisidian Antioch, we read this account: "As Paul and Barnabas were going out, the people kept begging that these things might be spoken to them the next Sabbath. Now when the meeting of the synagogue had broken up, many of the Jews and of the God-fearing proselytes followed Paul and Barnabas, who, speaking to them, were urging them to continue in the grace of God." (Acts 13:42-43) Here we find mentioned both Jewish groups in the synagogue – the natural-born Jews and "the God-fearing proselytes" (synagogue members who had made a full conversion to Judaism). But since Paul addressed "those who fear God" at the start of his message, all three groups existed in the synagogue in Pisidian Antioch. The truth is that whenever Paul went into a synagogue in the diaspora, he believed that he was taking the gospel message to Gentiles as well as Jews.

Paul and Barnabas continued going to Jewish synagogues throughout their first missionary journey. "In Iconium they entered the synagogue of the Jews together, and spoke in such a manner that a large number of people believed, both of Jews and of Greeks." (Acts 14:1) Since the "Greeks" were in the synagogue, they had to be God-fearers. So when the Bible records that both Jews and Greeks believed, it means that both Jews and Gentiles accepted the gospel. This was all accomplished by going to the Jewish synagogue in Iconium.

What about when Paul went on later missionary journeys? Did he change his pattern after the council in Jerusalem recorded in Acts 15? In Philippi, Paul went out to a riverside on the Sabbath to talk to people. Why? There must not have been a synagogue in Philippi. But he went out "to a riverside, where we were supposing that there would be a place of prayer." (Acts 16:13) Who would be praying at a riverside on the Sabbath? Not a bunch of sun-worshipping Greeks or Romans. The people who would be praying at a riverside on the Sabbath would be natural-born Jews, proselytes to Judaism, and God-fearers who accepted Jewish moral teachings – the same three groups to whom Paul reached out in the synagogue.

In Acts 17 we read the account of Paul in Thessalonica. "Now when they had traveled through Amphipolis and Apolonia, they came to Thessalonica, where there was a synagogue of the Jews. And according to Paul's custom, he went into them, and for three Sabbath days reasoned with them from the Scriptures."

(Acts 17:1-2) First, let us note that Paul didn't stop to preach in Amphipolis or Apolonia. Why? My guess is that there was no synagogue in either Amphipolis or Apolonia. But there was a synagogue in Thessalonica and Paul stopped to preach there.

Furthermore, the Scripture in Acts 17:2 records that "for three Sabbath days" Paul "reasoned with them from the Scriptures." Most of the Gentiles didn't attend synagogue services. Why didn't he reach out to them on Sunday or some other day of the week? But he didn't because the Gentiles he was trying to reach first were in the synagogue. Paul always tried to reach the natural-born Jews, proselytes to Judaism, and God-fearing Gentiles first.

Finally, when Paul was in Corinth, the Bible records: "And he was reasoning in the synagogue every Sabbath and trying to persuade Jews and Greeks." (Acts 18:4) Where were the Greeks that Paul was trying to persuade? "In the synagogue." As we have seen, the Greeks in the synagogue were God-fearers; they accepted the moral teachings of Judaism, but not circumcision. So the Jews in the synagogue still considered these God-fearers Greeks. As Paul did throughout his missionary journeys, he endeavored to reach the Greeks in the synagogue.

Did Paul reach Gentiles outside of the synagogue? Definitely yes. At Lystra Paul reached a lame man whom the Lord used Paul to heal. "The crowds" mentioned when this healing took place (see Acts 14:11) seem to indicate that this event occurred outdoors. So in all likelihood, this man was a Gentile with no connection to Judaism. Similarly in Acts 16 Paul and Silas reached the Philippian jailer, most likely a Greek or a Roman with no teaching in Judaism. However, these were the exceptions recorded in Acts chapters 13 through 18. The vast majority of the Gentiles whom Paul reached with the gospel on his missionary journeys were God-fearers involved in Jewish synagogues.

CHAPTER 6

HOW NEW TESTAMENT WRITERS VIEWED THE SCRIPTURES

How did New Testament writers view the Scriptures? First, let's establish what the Scriptures were when the New Testament writers wrote. There was no New Testament when the New Testament writers wrote the gospels, Acts, the epistles, and Revelation. At that time the only books which they recognized as Scriptures were the writings of the Old Testament. Paul wrote: "All Scripture is given by inspiration of God." (II Timothy 3:16 KJV) The Scripture to which Paul refers in this verse is the Old Testament." Peter wrote: "Being born again, not of corruptible seed, but of incorruptible, by the word of God, which liveth and abideth forever." (I Peter 1:23 KJV) The Word of God to which Peter refers in this verse is the Old Testament.

Let's start with the gospel of Matthew. Matthew repeatedly quoted Old Testament verses that Jesus Christ fulfilled to prove that Jesus Christ was indeed the Lord and Savior which the Old Testament prophets predicted Him to be. I will take just three examples from the first two chapters of Matthew. After recounting that Mary was with child by the Holy Spirit (Matthew 1:18b), Matthew wrote: "Now all this took place to fulfill what was spoken by the Lord through the prophet: 'BEHOLD, THE VIRGIN SHALL BE WITH CHILD AND SHALL BEAR A SON, AND THEY SHALL CALL HIS NAME IMMANUEL,' which translated means, 'God with us.'"

(Mathew 1:22-23) Again Matthew wrote: "So Joseph got up and took the Child and His mother while it was still night, and left for Egypt. He remained there until the death of Herod. This was to fulfill what had been spoken by the LORD through the prophet: 'OUT OF EGYPT I CALLED MY SON.'" (Matthew 2:14-15) Then Matthew recorded how Herod killed all the male infants in Bethlehem. (Matthew 2:16) "Then what had been spoken through Jeremiah the prophet was fulfilled: 'A VOICE WAS HEARD IN RAMAH, WEEPING AND GREAT MOURNING, RACHEL WEEPING FOR HER CHILDREN; AND SHE REFUSED TO BE COMFORTED, BECAUSE THEY WERE NO MORE.'" (Matthew 2:17-18)

I gave all the quotes above from the New American Standard version for a reason. The NAS capitalizes Old Testament quotes recorded in the New Testament. For the record, the three Old Testament Scriptures quoted by Matthew above are found in Isaiah 7:14, Hosea 11:1, and Jeremiah 31:15 respectively. Matthew would not have quoted all these Old Testament Scriptures if he did not regard them as authoritative. But Matthew did regard the Old Testament Scriptures as authoritative and so he quoted them throughout his gospel. Mark and Luke also frequently quoted Old Testament Scriptures in their gospels. (For examples, see Mark 1:2-3, Mark 7:6-7, Luke 4:17-19, and Luke 10:26-27.) Of the gospel writers, only John did not quote much from the Old Testament because he focused more on what Jesus said while He was here on earth.

Did the apostles continue treating the Old Testament as authoritative in the Book of Acts? In Acts 1:20 Peter made the case that another apostle needed to be chosen to replace Judas. He made this case by quoting two verses from the Old Testament: "For it is written in the book of Psalms, 'LET HIS HOMESTEAD BE DESOLATE, AND LET NO ONE DWELL IN IT'; and 'LET ANOTHER TAKE HIS OFFICE.'" (Acts 1:20) The verses Peter quoted were Psalm 69:25 and Psalm 109:8. Peter would not have quoted these verses in regard to a replacement for Judas unless he believed that they were authoritative for the decision to be made. Similarly, Peter quoted Joel 2:28-32 in Acts 2:17-21 to explain what happened on the day of Pentecost. He would not have done so unless he believed that the passage in Joel was authoritative for explaining what happened in Jerusalem that day. There are many other examples of the apostles quoting the Old Testament in Acts. The point is that the apostles quoted the Old Testament throughout Acts because they believed that the Old Testament Scriptures were the Word of God.

Now some Christians believe that the Old Testament was done away with by the council in Jerusalem recorded in Acts 15. We will take up the council in Jerusalem in a later chapter. At this point, we will just note that the New Testament writers of the epistles continued to quote the Old Testament after the council in Jerusalem. If the Old Testament were done away with at the council in Jerusalem, there would be no further need for the New Testament writers to quote the Old Testament. But they continued to do so.

Let's start with the book of Romans, a book from which some quote (out of context) to say that the Old Testament has been done away with. Consider the following Scriptures where Paul quoted the Old Testament in Romans. "For in it the righteousness of God is revealed from faith to faith; as it is written, 'BUT THE RIGHTEOUS man SHALL LIVE BY FAITH.'" (Romans 1:17) What then? Are we better than they? Not at all; for we have already charged that both Jews and Greeks are all under sin; as it is written, 'THERE IS NONE RIGHTEOUS, NOT EVEN ONE.'" (Romans 3:9-10) "For what does the Scripture say, 'ABRAHAM BELIEVED GOD, AND IT WAS CREDITED TO HIM AS RIGHTEOUSNESS.'" (Romans 4:3) "Owe nothing to anyone except to love one another; for he who loves his neighbor has fulfilled the law. For this, 'YOU SHALL NOT COMMIT ADULTERY, YOU SHALL NOT MURDER, YOU SHALL NOT STEAL, YOU SHALL NOT COVET,' and if there is any other commandment, it is summed up in this saying, 'YOU SHALL LOVE YOUR NEIGHBOR AS YOURSELF.'" (Romans 13:8-9) Paul gave other Old Testament quotes in his epistle to the Romans. The point again is this: Paul would not have repeatedly quoted the Old Testament if he did not regard it as authoritative Scripture.

Now please note the last quote from Romans given in the paragraph above. In Romans 13:9 Paul quoted in order the 7th commandment, the 6th commandment, the 8th commandment, and the 10th commandment. (In the King James Version the 9th commandment is also included in the quote.) So in this verse Paul quoted at least four of the Ten Commandments. At this point in his letter to the Romans he had already shown them that they couldn't become righteous by the law (Romans chapter 3) or remain righteous by the law (Romans chapter 7). Yet obviously Paul didn't believe that the law was done away with if he was quoting it as an example of loving behavior. In fact, he concluded Romans 13:9 by quoting Leviticus 19:18: "YOU SHALL LOVE YOUR NEIGHBOR AS YOURSELF."

Paul quoted many other Old Testament Scriptures throughout his epistles. I will give just two more examples from epistles other than Romans. "For He says, 'AT THE ACCEPTABLE TIME I LISTENED TO YOU, AND ON THE DAY OF SALVATION I HELPED YOU." (II Corinthians 6:2) This is a quote from Isaiah 49:8. Again in Galatians 4:30 Paul wrote: "But what does the Scripture say? 'CAST OUT THE BONDWOMAN AND HER SON, FOR THE SON OF THE BONDWOMAN SHALL NOT BE AN HEIR WITH THE SON OF THE FREE WOMAN.'" This is a quote from Genesis 21:10. Why did Paul keep quoting from the Old Testament Scriptures throughout his letters? Because he regarded them as the authoritative Word of God.

Let's also consider Peter's view of the Old Testament Scriptures. Peter wrote: "For you have been born again not of seed which is perishable but imperishable, that is, through the living and enduring word of God. For, 'ALL FLESH IS AS GRASS, AND ALL ITS GLORY LIKE THE FLOWER OF GRASS, THE GRASS WITHERS, AND THE FLOWER FALLS OFF, BUT THE WORD OF THE LORD ENDURES FOREVER.' And this is the word which was preached to you." (I Peter 1:23-25) In this passage Peter quoted from Isaiah 40:6-8. Again Peter wrote: "For this is contained in Scripture: 'BEHOLD, I LAY IN ZION A CHOICE STONE, A PRECIOUS CORNER stone, AND HE WHO BELIEVES IN HIM WILL NOT BE DISAPPOINTED." (I Peter 2:6) Here Peter quoted from Isaiah 28:16. As we noted with Paul, so we note with Peter. Peter quoted Old

Testament Scriptures because he believed that they were "the living and enduring word of God."

The truth is that all the New Testament writers believed that the Scriptures of the Old Testament were the Word of God. Did they believe that some of the Old Testament Scriptures were fulfilled in Jesus Christ? Yes, they did. Did they believe that the old covenant laid out in the Old Testament was replaced by the new covenant? Yes, they did. But from their many quotes from the Old Testament, it is clear that the New Testament writers regarded the Old Testament as the Word of God. They believed that "all Scripture is inspired by God." (II Timohy 3:16) Moreover, when Paul wrote II Timothy 3:16, "all Scripture" was the Old Testament.

CHAPTER 7

HOW NEW TESTAMENT WRITERS VIEWED THE COMMANDMENTS

In the previous chapter, we saw that the writers of the New Testament viewed the Old Testament as Scripture. A few modern Christians have taken the view that although the New Testament writers looked at the history books, the poetry books, and the writings of the prophets as Scripture, they did not similarly look at the books of the law as Scripture. Many more have taken the view that although the first five books of the Bible are Scripture, the New Testament writers did not look at the specific parts of those books in which commandments, statutes, judgments, and ordinances are laid out as Scripture. For the purpose of definition, the books of the law are the first five books of the Bible – Genesis, Exodus, Leviticus, Numbers, and Deuteronomy.

How did the New Testament writers view the law? Did they share the view held by many modern Christians that the law is done away with? Or did they view parts of the law as done away while viewing other parts of the law as not done away with? Terminology is part of our problem here. From the New Testament, it is clear that they believed certain parts of the law were fulfilled in Jesus Christ. As we shall see in this chapter, the New Testament writers also believed that certain parts of the law were just as much in force after Christ's death as before His death.

Now some of you who are reading this have been so programmed that the law is done away with that you are ready to stop reading this book right now. Your problem is probably the same as mine was: my programmed view of the law was entirely based on verses quoted out of context. You can prove almost anything if you pull verses out of context. But if you put those verses back into their context, then their meaning is determined by the context.

Let's start with the words of Jesus Himself. Jesus is the final authority in matters of doctrine in His church. Regarding the law, Jesus said: "Do not think that I came to destroy the Law or the Prophets; I did not come to abolish but to fulfill. For truly I say to you, until heaven and earth pass away, not the smallest letter or stroke shall pass from the Law until all is accomplished. Whoever then annuls one of the least of these commandments, and teaches others to do the same, shall be called least in the kingdom of heaven; but whoever keeps and teaches them, he shall be called great in the kingdom of heaven." (Matthew 5:17-19) Jesus declared that He didn't come "to destroy the Law." Rather, He came to "fulfill" the law. Now some have taken this to mean that when Jesus died, He fulfilled the law. Consequently, they believe that the law is now done away with. But Jesus said: "Until heaven and earth pass away, not the smallest letter or stroke shall pass from the Law." Since heaven and earth have not yet passed away, then the law must still be in effect. Finally, Jesus qualified His statements about the law by emphasizing that the commandments are still in effect.

Part of our problem here is that we don't understand the law the way that 1st Century Jewish Christians did. Basically, the law consists of four parts:

commandments, statutes, judgments, and ordinances. The law also contained testimonies, but testimonies just testified of what God did through men. (For example, the crossing of the Red Sea is a testimony of the power of God to deliver His people.) Now refer back to what Jesus declared in Matthew 5:17-19. Jesus emphasized that the commandments remained in effect. He did not similarly emphasize the statures, judgments, and ordinances. So from Christ's own words the most important part of the law was the commandments.

Did other New Testament writers retain the same view of the commandments contained in the law? Paul wrote: "Circumcision is nothing, and uncircumcision is nothing, but what matters is the keeping of the commandments of God," (I Corinthians 7:19) If Paul believed that the law was done away with, he would not have written that "what matters is the keeping of the commandments of God." Moreover, Paul did not write "the commandments of Jesus"; he wrote "the commandments of God." The statement "the commandments of God" is a clear reference to the commandments contained in the law and particularly to the Ten Commandments.

Similarly, Peter wrote: "For it would have been better for them not to have known the way of righteousness, than having known it, to turn away from the holy commandment handed on to them." (II Peter 2:21) From the context in II Peter, it is not clear whether Peter was referring to the commandments of the law or the commandments of Jesus in this verse. But Jesus based His commandments on the commandments in the law. (See Matthew chapter 5 in this regard.) The point is that Peter, like Paul, still viewed commandments as important.

Likewise, John wrote: "By this we know that we love the children of God, when we love God and observe His commandments. For this is the love of God, that we keep His commandments; and His commandments are not burdensome." (I John 5:2-3) How do we know that we love God? "When we love God and observe His commandments." In fact, what is the love of God? "For this is the love of God, that we keep His commandments." Since the love of God is defined by keeping His commandments, we can rest assured that God's commandments are not done away with. All the New Testament apostles agreed with Jesus: the commandments of God are still in full force.

Finally, in Revelation we read: "So the dragon was enraged with the woman, and went off to make war with the rest of her children, who keep the commandments of God and hold the testimony of Jesus." (Revelation 12:17) Right down to the end of the Scriptures we find God's children keeping His commandments. Now some believe that Revelation 12 refers to natural Israel rather than the church. The problem is that Jews (natural Israel) don't "hold the testimony of Jesus." Only believers in Jesus maintain the testimony of Jesus. But according to this Scripture, they also "keep the commandments of God."

Now in closing this chapter, I need to emphasize that the New Testament writers did not believe that anyone could be saved by keeping God's commandments. In fact, I believe that they saw the commandments in relation to salvation the other way around – that is, that believers in Jesus Christ kept the commandments because they were saved. I will not belabor this point here. However, I will quote one New Testament passage that brings out the whole truth of salvation by grace followed by obedience to God's commandments. "For by grace you have been saved through faith; and that not of yourselves, it is the gift of God; not as a result of works, so that no one may boast. For we are His workmanship, created in Christ Jesus for good works, which God prepared beforehand so that we would walk in them." (Ephesians 2:8-10) Many believers quote Ephesians 2:8-9, but few quote Ephesians 2:10 along with verses 8 and 9. When Paul spoke of works, he was almost always referring to the works of the law. In Ephesians 2:8-10 Paul made it clear that we are saved by grace without the works of the law. But then he stated that salvation by grace is followed by a life of doing good works. Works in verse 10 is the same Greek word as works in verse 9. Salvation by grace, then, leads to a life of doing good works – that is, to a life of obeying God's commandments.

CHAPTER 8

HOW NEW TESTAMENT WRITERS VIEWED THE ORDINANCES

In the previous chapter, we saw that the New Testament writers viewed the commandments given in the law as still in full force. Did they view the ordinances the same way? Absolutely not. The New Testament writers viewed the ordinances as fulfilled in Jesus Christ. We will look at two Scriptures written by the apostle Paul to confirm that they did not view the ordinances the same as they did the commandments.

"For He Himself is our peace, who has made both groups into one and broke down the barrier of the dividing wall, by abolishing in His flesh the enmity, which is the Law of commandments contained in ordinances, so that in Himself He might make the two into one new man, thus establishing peace." (Ephesians 2:14-15) In context, the two groups to whom Paul is referring in this passage are Jews and Gentiles. Basically, he is saying that God has brought these two groups together through the work of the cross. Specifically, they have been brought together by "abolishing in His flesh... the Law of commandments contained in ordinances." Many have misquoted this verse to affirm that the whole law is done away with. However, according to Ephesians 2:15 only the commandments contained in ordinances are abolished in Christ.

"When you were dead in your transgressions and the uncircumcision of your flesh, He made you alive together with Him, having forgiven us all our transgressions, having canceled out the certificate of debt consisting of decrees against us, which was hostile to us, and He has taken it out of the way, having nailed it to the cross." (Colossians 2:13-14) The word translated "decrees" in Colossians 2:14 is the same Greek word translated "ordinances" in Ephesians 2:15. The Greek word is *dogma*; it means ordinance. (For the record, the King James Version translates *dogma* as "ordinances" in Colossians 2:14.) Colossians 2:14 tells us the same thing as Ephesians 2:15: the ordinances were nailed to the cross with Christ. Unlike the commandments, which all the New Testament writers confirm as still in force, the ordinances were abolished because they were fulfilled in Jesus Christ.

According to the Scriptures, what are the ordinances? Actually, the writer of the Epistle to the Hebrews gives us a very clear answer. "Now even the first covenant had regulations of divine worship and the earthly sanctuary." (Hebrews 9:1) The King James Version translates this same verse: "Then verily the first covenant had also ordinances of divine service, and a worldly sanctuary." The Greek word translated "regulations" in the NAS and "ordinances" in the KJV is *dikaioma*. It literally means a judicial appointment. But as we see from Hebrews chapter 9, that's what ordinances are – judicial appointments for carrying out the various aspects of the "divine worship" in "the earthly sanctuary." Read through Hebrews chapter 9 and you will see that the ordinances consisted basically of three areas of regulation of the divine worship in the Old Testament. The ordinances included the animal sacrifices, the regulations of the Levitical priesthood, and the regulations of the tabernacle (which carried over into the temple).

"But when Christ appeared as a high priest of the good things to come, He entered through the greater and more perfect tabernacle, not made with hands, that is to say, not of this creation; and not through the blood of goats and calves, but through His own blood, He entered the holy place once for all, having obtained eternal redemption. For if the blood of goats and bulls and the ashes of a heifer sprinkling those who have been defiled sanctify for the cleansing of the flesh, how much more will the blood of Christ, who through the eternal Spirit offered Himself without blemish to God, cleanse your conscience from dead works to serve the living God?" (Hebrews 9:11-14) The blood of Christ replaced the blood of all the animal sacrifices of the old covenant. The ordinances of animal sacrifices were all replaced by the sacrifice of Jesus Christ Himself.

"For Christ did not enter a holy place made with hands, a mere copy of the true one, but into heaven itself, now to appear in the presence of God for us; nor was it that He would offer Himself often, as the high priest entered the holy place year by year with blood that is not his own." (Hebrews 9:24-25) Jesus Christ replaced the Levitical priesthood of the old covenant. The Levitical priests had to make sacrifices every year, but Jesus Christ made one sacrifice for all mankind. Besides, He is now in heaven making intercession for us. No Levitical priest ever made intercession for us in heaven.

"For there was a tabernacle prepared, the outer one, in which were the lampstand and the table and the sacred bread; this is called the holy place. Behind the second veil, there was a tabernacle which is called the Holy of Holies, having a golden altar of incense and the ark covered on all sides with gold, in which was a golden jar holding the manna, and Aaron's rod which budded, and the tables of the covenant; and above it were the cherubim of glory overshadowing the mercy seat; but of these things we cannot now speak in detail." (Hebrews 9:2-5) The tabernacle and the things in it were the first things enumerated by the writer of Hebrews after mentioning the ordinances. (Hebrews 9:1) The New Testament writers affirmed that Jesus Himself is our tabernacle now. "For we know that if the earthly tent which is our house is torn down, we have a building from God, a house not made with hands, eternal in the heavens." (II Corinthians 5:1) Both the tabernacle and the temple have been torn down. But the tabernacle of Jesus Himself replaced the ordinances of the Old Testament tabernacle.

Now let us look at another passage in Hebrews where the writer affirmed that the law had changed. "Now if perfection was through the Levitical priesthood (for on the basis of it the people received the Law), what further need was there for another priest to arise after the order of Melchizedek, and not be designated according to the order of Aaron? For when the priesthood is changed, of necessity there takes place a change of law also." (Hebrews 7:11-12) Does this Scripture say that the law was done away with? No, but it does tell us that the law was changed. In context, the law of the priesthood was changed. As we have already noted, Hebrews chapter 9 backs this up. All of the ordinances were fulfilled in Christ; so the law of the ordinances was abolished in Christ.

The New Testament also records that the ordinance of circumcision was abolished in Christ. There are many New Testament Scriptures which make this point. I will quote just one Scripture in this regard because this Scripture not only brings out that circumcision has been done away with, but also that it has been replaced by water baptism. "And in Him you were also circumcised with a circumcision made without hands, in the removal of the body of the flesh by the circumcision of Christ, having been buried with Him in baptism, in which you were also raised up with Him through faith in the working of God, who raised Him from the dead." (Colossians 2:11-12)

All this being declared in regard to the ordinances, you cannot find any statement in Hebrews asserting that the commandments were fulfilled in Christ. As we saw in the previous chapter, all the New Testament writers viewed the commandments as still in force. They just didn't view the commandments as the instrument of righteousness – either for becoming righteous or for remaining righteous.

Finally, the law included the statutes and judgments as well as the commandments and ordinances. How did the New Testament writers view the statutes and judgments? Actually, the New Testament doesn't answer this question because the New Testament writers never discuss the statutes and judgments as they do the commandments and ordinances. However, there is a good possibility that they viewed the judgments as abolished in Christ. Some of the judgments contained curses. In this regard, Paul wrote: "Christ has redeemed us from the curse of the Law, having become a curse for us – for it is written, 'CURSED IS EVERYONE WHO HANGS ON A TREE.'" (Galatians 3:13) Christ hung on the tree of the cross for us, and in doing so bore the curse of the law for us. In consequence, we have been redeemed from any judgments that contained curses through Christ's death on the cross.

CHAPTER 9

THE JERUSALEM COUNCIL

Now we come to Acts 15 – the record of the Jerusalem council. I personally believe that this is one of the most misinterpreted chapters in the Bible. Why? Because most of those who attempt to interpret the record of the Jerusalem council in Acts 15 ignore the 1st Century context in which it was set. From our previous chapters let's review what we have already learned about the New Testament church and its writers. First, all the writers of the New Testament were Jews. In fact, all the early leaders in the New Testament church were Jews. Yes, they were converted Jews who had accepted Jesus Christ as their Lord and Savior. But what we have already noted is that they still considered themselves Jews. So let us recognize that all the participants in the Jerusalem council were Jews – converted Jews who believed in Jesus Christ. Not one converted Gentile participated in the Jerusalem council.

    Second, we have noted that all these Jews still went to the temple or the synagogue. If they were in Jerusalem, they went to the temple. And if they were in the diaspora, they went to the synagogue. They also had house church meetings of their own, but we will take up early Christian house church meetings in a later chapter. As we have seen, even in Paul's missionary journeys Paul and those who accompanied him repeatedly went to synagogues. They did this because they could reach both Jews (natural-born Jews and proselytes) and God-fearers

(Gentiles who regularly attended synagogue services) in the synagogue.

Third, we have seen that although these Jews viewed the ordinances of the law as fulfilled in Christ, they did not view the commandments of the law the same way. In the chapter on the commandments, I quoted Scriptures written by Peter, Paul, and John to show that none of them viewed the commandments as done away with. The truth is Paul, Peter, and John all wrote their epistles after the Jerusalem council. Those who interpret Acts 15 to affirm that all the law is done away with are at odds with the writers of the New Testament.

Acts 15 begins as follows: "Some men came down for Judea and began teaching the brethren, 'Unless you are circumcised according to the law of Moses, you cannot be saved.' And when Paul and Barnabas had great dissension and debate with them, the brethren determined that Paul and Barnabas and some others of them should go up to Jerusalem to the apostles and elders concerning this matter." (Acts 15:1-2) Acts 15 starts with men coming to Antioch from Judea and teaching that circumcision was required for salvation. This was the issue that Paul and Barnabas took to the council in Jerusalem: Was circumcision required for salvation? That this was the issue is also confirmed by Acts 15:5: "But some of the sect of the Pharisees who had believed stood up, saying, 'It is necessary to circumcise them and to direct them to observe the law of Moses.'" Here they expanded the issue to include keeping the law of Moses to be saved. But in context that is all that the issue was - whether you had to be circumcised and keep the law of Moses to be saved. Observing the law of Moses was not the issue. Observing the law of Moses in order to be saved was the issue. This is consistent with what we have already noted because all the participants in the Jerusalem council observed the commandments in the law.

Was circumcision required for salvation? The answer of the Jerusalem council was emphatically "No." Peter gave the decisive words on this issue: 'Now therefore why do you put God to the test by placing a yoke upon the neck of the disciples, a yoke which neither our fathers nor we have been able to bear? But we believe that we are saved through the grace of the Lord Jesus, in the same way as they also are." (Acts 15:10-11) Peter stated unequivocally that we are saved by grace without circumcision or observing the law of Moses. To this statement the whole council in Jerusalem agreed.

Then James stood up and spoke: "Brethren, listen to me. Simeon (Peter) has related how God first concerned Himself about taking from among the Gentiles a people for His name." (Acts 15:13-14) After quoting from the prophets, James then declared: "Therefore it is my judgment that we do not trouble those who are turning to God from among the Gentiles." (Acts 15:19) Here James expressed his agreement with Peter – that circumcision and keeping the law of Moses were not necessary for salvation.

Then James continued: "But that we write to them that they abstain from things contaminated by idols and from fornication and from what is strangled and from blood." (James 5:20) Many Christian writers have pulled this verse out of context to affirm that the law was at that point done away with for Gentiles. But the context was whether they had to keep any of the law of Moses to be saved. All the participants in the Jerusalem council observed the commandments of the law of Moses. They affirmed keeping the commandments throughout the New Testament. In context, James was saying that the Gentiles were saved by grace, but that they still should observe abstaining from things contaminated by idols, from fornication, from what is strangled, and from blood. Why James chose these four particular things I don't know. Did the Gentiles have to keep any of these things to be saved? No, the Jerusalem council had already agreed that men were saved by grace without keeping any of the law.

So why did James suggest these four things as requirements for the Gentiles? In the context of what we know about the New Testament church, I see only two possible answers to this question. First, James could have believed that failure to observe these prohibitions might have resulted in weakened consciences where believers questioned their salvation. Things offered to idols were discussed more than once in the New Testament; so this was a big issue in the 1st Century church. Second, since the Pharisees who believed in Christ lost their argument in Acts 15, James may have been offering them a sop. Since circumcision and keeping the law of Moses clearly were not required for salvation, throwing in four things from the law didn't make them requirements for salvation either. Why did Paul and Barnabas agree to this? Because they knew that they were going to continue teaching salvation by grace without any works of the law to the Gentiles. Yes, they delivered the decrees on which the Jerusalem council agreed to the churches of the Gentiles (Acts 16:4), but that is the last we hear of this matter.

Now I will quote the verse that most of the interpreters of Acts 15 overlook: "For Moses from ancient generations has in every city those who preach him, since he is read in the synagogues every Sabbath." (Acts 15:21)

From Paul and Barnabas relating how God had used them among the Gentiles (Acts 15:12), James knew that Paul and Barnabas were going to synagogues among the Gentiles. Plus, he knew that they were still encouraging Gentile converts to attend synagogue services. (As we have already noted, many of these Gentile converts were already God-fearers in synagogues.) So James believed that the Gentile converts in the diaspora would continue attending synagogue services. Why was this important to James? Because the law of Moses was "read in the synagogues every Sabbath." James firmly believed that Gentile converts would continue to hear the law of Moses every Sabbath in synagogues.

Knowing that James was upholding the reading of the law in synagogue services completely negates the idea that the law was done away with at the Jerusalem council recorded in Acts 15. The Jerusalem council affirmed that salvation was by grace without any works of the law of Moses. But the Jerusalem council did not do away with the law. In the next chapter we will take an overview of the how the New Testament writers viewed the law in total by examining Paul's coverage of this subject in his epistle to the Romans.

CHAPTER 10

THE NEW TESTAMENT WRITERS' OVERALL VIEW OF THE LAW

We have looked at how the New Testament writers viewed the commandments. Moreover, we have looked at how they viewed the ordinances. Plus, we have seen that the decisions of the Jerusalem council were consistent with the New Testament writers' view of the law. In this chapter, we shall attempt to summarize their view of the law. The apostle Paul gives a complete overview of the law in his Epistle to the Romans. So that is where we will go to ascertain the New Testament writers' overall view of the law.

"Now we know that whatever the Law says, it speaks to those who are under the Law, so that every mouth may be closed and all the world may become accountable to God; because by the works of the Law no flesh will be justified in His sight; for through the Law comes the knowledge of sin." (Romans 3:19-20) Paul begins his discussion of faith and the law by telling us that "through the Law comes the knowledge of sin." The law convicts us of our sin. Paul gives an example of the law's conviction of sin in Romans 7:7: "What shall we say then? Is the Law sin? May it never be! On the contrary, I would not have come to know sin except through the Law; for I would not have known about coveting if the Law had not said, 'YOU SHALL NOT COVET.'" Paul quotes the tenth commandment as an example of the law convicting him of sin. In essence, the law makes us accountable to God by convicting us of our sin.

Do other New Testament writers agree with Paul's view in this regard. John declares: "Everyone who practices sin also practices lawlessness and sin is lawlessness." (I John 3:4) Since sin is lawlessness, then it is the law that convicts of us of our sin. John is in agreement with Paul that one purpose of the law is to convict us of our sin.

Returning to Romans 3, Paul continues: "But now apart from the Law the righteousness of God has been manifested, being witnessed by the Law and the Prophets, even the righteousness of God through faith in Jesus Christ for all those who believe; for there is no difference." (Romans 3:21-22) The Jews who didn't believe in Jesus still thought that they had to keep the law to be justified before God. But these New Testament Jews who had found Jesus Christ as their Lord and Savior had learned otherwise. They had come to know that they were justified by faith without any works of the law. Paul carries this thought out until he makes his summary statement in Romans 3:28: "For we maintain that a man is justified by faith apart from the works of the Law." The New Testament writers clearly believed that no one could be justified from sin by any works of the law.

Romans chapters 6-8 is a three-chapter discussion of how to get the victory over sin. In summary, Romans chapter 6 informs us that we start getting the victory over sin through reckoning our old sin nature dead with Jesus on the cross. Romans chapter 7 then tells us that we cannot get the victory over sin through keeping the law. Finally, Romans chapter 8 teaches us that we must follow the leading of the Holy Spirit to get the complete victory over sin. One verse from Romans 7 has often been quoted out of its context to say that the law has been entirely done away with. But this interpretation is at odds not only with the whole New Testament, but also with the whole Epistle to the Romans.

"But now we have been released from the Law, having died to that by which we were bound, so that we serve in newness of the Spirit and not in oldness of the letter." (Romans 7:6) This verse clearly states that "we have been released from the Law." Taken out of context, it seems to say that the law is entirely done away with. In context, however, it means that we have been released from the law for getting the victory over sin. Paul knew that the tendency of Jewish believers in Christ was to revert to the law to try to get the victory over sin. In Romans 7 Paul repeatedly tells them that they will never get the victory over sin through keeping the law.

Moreover, if Romans 7:6 is indeed teaching that the law is done away with, it is at odds with other verses in the same chapter. The very next verse (Romans 7:7) shows us that we learn from the law that coveting is sin. If the law is entirely done away with, then we have no way of knowing that covetousness is sin. Further, in Romans 7:12 Paul declares: "So then, the Law is holy, and the commandment is holy and righteous and good." If the law is entirely done away with in Romans 7:6, Paul would not write six verses later that "the Law is holy."

In effect, a good summary of Romans chapter 3 together with Romans chapter 7 is as follows: In Romans 3 Paul first teaches that the law convicts us of sin. Then he goes on to teach that we cannot get saved and become righteous by the law. In Romans 7 Paul further teaches that we cannot get the victory over sin and remain righteous by the law. So at this point in Romans, Paul has taught us that the law is still in effect for the knowledge of sin, but that it is not in effect at all for getting saved and becoming righteous or for getting the victory over sin and remaining righteous. Paul sums this all up in Romans 10:4: "For Christ is the end of the law for righteousness to everyone who believes." Paul doesn't state that Christ is the end of law. He states that "Christ is the end of the law for righteousness."

Finally, in Romans 13 Paul affirms one more purpose of the law. "Owe nothing to anyone except to love one another; for he who loves his neighbor has fulfilled the Law. For this, 'YOU SHALL NOT COMMIT ADULTERY, YOU SHALL NOT MURDER, YOU SHALL NOT STEAL, YOU SHALL NOT COVET,' and if there is any other commandment, it is summed up in this saying, 'YOU SHALL LOVE YOUR NEIGHBOR AS YOURSELF.' Love does no wrong to a neighbor; therefore love is the fulfillment of the law." (Romans 13:8-10) "Love is the fulfillment of the law." When the Holy Spirit leads you to love others, the Holy Spirit guides you not to commit adultery, not to murder, not to steal, and not to covet. In Romans 13:9 Paul quotes the seventh, sixth, eighth, and tenth commandments (in order) to demonstrate that when we keep these commandments, we show love to one another. In fact, he closes the verse by quoting Leviticus 19:18: "YOU SHALL LOVE YOUR NEIGHBOR AS YOURSELF." If the law is entirely done away with, then loving your neighbor as yourself is not in effect today.

What's Paul's point? The Holy Spirit leads us to walk in love. And how do we know when we are walking in love? We know that we are walking in love when we keep God's commandments. That's what Paul is teaching in Romans 13:8-10. When you walk in love, you fulfill the law; and you know that you are fulfilling the law when you keep God's commandments. The apostle John teaches the same truth this way: "By this we know that we love the children of God, when we love God and observe His commandments. For this is the love of God, that we keep His commandments; and His commandments are not burdensome." (I John 5:2-3)

In summary, then, the New Testament writers viewed the law as done away with either for becoming righteous or for remaining righteous. However, they saw the law as giving us the knowledge of sin. Plus, they viewed the keeping of the law as proof that they were walking in love when they followed the leading of the Holy Spirit.

CHAPTER 11

TWO VERSES OF PARTICULAR INTEREST

In this chapter, I take up two verses on which the New Testament writers had a different perspective than do most Christians today. Recall in Chapter 3 that we looked at the New Testament writers' perception of time. Recall that they followed Biblical time right down the line. The Biblical day starts at sundown and ends the following sundown. The Biblical week starts at sundown on the first day of the Biblical week and ends just before sundown on the seventh day of the Biblical week. The Biblical month starts on the new moon and ends on the day before the next new moon. None of these examples equate to Roman time perceptions. Yet that is what we have been trained to think in all our lives – the Roman perception of time.

When did the first day of the week begin in the minds of the New Testament writers? In Biblical time it began at sundown on Saturday evening. On the average, then, the first day of the Biblical week started six hours before the first day of the Roman week began. In consequence, on average the Biblical week likewise started six hours before the Roman week began. So if an event happened on the first of the week, that event took place on Saturday evening in Roman time. Similarly, if an event commenced on the first day of the week and lasted until midnight, that event took place on Saturday evening in Roman time. To have the same perspective as the New Testament writers did, we need to get this into our thinking. Their week and the first day of their week did not start at midnight at the beginning of Sunday. Their week and the first day of their week started at sundown on Saturday evening.

"On the first day of the week, when we were gathered together to break bread, Paul began talking to them, intending to leave the next day, and he prolonged his message until midnight." (Acts 20:7) Many Christians have cited this verse as proof that the early church met on Sunday. Their Roman thinking takes over and they misinterpret this verse in agreement with their Roman thinking. This meeting did take place "on the first day of the week." But was this meeting on Saturday evening or on Sunday daytime in Roman time? The verse tells us that Paul "prolonged his message until midnight." For this meeting to be on the first day of the week and for Paul to continue his message until midnight on the first day of this week means that this meeting took place on Saturday evening in Roman time. If this meeting had continued until midnight at the end of Sunday, the Bible would have said "on the second day of the week."

The truth is that some modern versions translate the first phrase in Acts 20:7 "on Saturday evening." These translations do this to help keep us from thinking about this verse in Roman time. No New Testament writer would have viewed this verse as referring to a daytime meeting on the first day of the week. Neither should we. The New Testament writers saw the meeting recorded in Acts 20:7 as an evening meeting on the first day of the week. In Roman time that means that this meeting occurred on Saturday evening.

Nevertheless, some have still argued that Acts 20:7 proves that the early church met to break bread on the first day of the week. In this case, the early church did meet to break bread on the first day of the week. The truth is that the Scriptures record that the early church met to break bread on every day of the week: "Day by day continuing with one accord in the temple, and breaking bread from house to house, they were taking their meals together with gladness and sincerity of heart." (Acts 2:46) In Acts 20:7 some members of the early church just happened to meet on Saturday evening on the first day of the week to break bread.

The second verse we will consider is I Corinthians 16:2: "On the first day of every week each one of you is to put aside and save, as he may prosper, so that no collections be made when I come." The King James Version translates this same verse as follows: "Upon the first *day* of the week let every one of you lay by him in store, as *God* hath prospered him, that there be no gatherings when I come." Please note that both the words *day* and *God* are in italics. That means that these words are not in the original Greek. Look up "day" in the concordance and you will find no reference for I Corinthians 16:2. That's because the word "day" is not used in I Corinthians 16:2. (Why the New American Standard translators did not put *day* in italics I don't know.) A better translation of the first phrase of this verse would be "On the first of every week" (NAS) or "Upon the first of the week." (KJV)

So when was the first of the week in Biblical time? At sundown on the first day of the Biblical week. So in Roman time that would be around 6 PM on Saturday evening. Get rid of your Roman time thinking here. Paul is exhorting the Corinthian Christians to set aside something for collections "on the first of every week" – that is, at sundown on Saturday evening in

Roman time. The first of the Biblical week is at sundown on Saturday evening in Roman time – not at midnight.

Now some argue that I Corinthians 16:2 gives evidence of a Sunday meeting. That is impossible since we have just shown that this verse refers to what Paul exhorted the Corinthian Christians to do on the first of the week – that is, at sundown on Saturday evening in Roman time. Plus, there is no mention of a meeting in I Corinthians 16:2. Paul just exhorted the Corinthians to set some money aside to give whenever collections were taken. We have been reading our Roman thinking into this verse for so long that it is very difficult for us to see that Sunday is not in this verse at all.

Now I make an overall observation on Acts 20:7 and I Corinthians 16:2. These are the two verses which modern Sunday keepers most often use in defense of Sunday being the holy day. But we have just shown that in Biblical time neither verse refers to the Roman Sunday. Both verses refer to the beginning of the Biblical week, which is at sundown on Saturday evening in Roman time. Correcting our thinking about time will definitely aid us in correctly interpreting the Scriptures.

To close this chapter, I encourage you to try to start thinking in Biblical time. Every evening at sundown think this is the beginning of another day in God's calendar. If it's sundown on Monday evening, don't think this is the last part of Monday. Instead, think that this is the beginning of the third day of the week. Similarly, if it's sundown on Friday evening, don't think this is the last part of Friday. Instead, think that this is the beginning of the seventh day of the week. Better yet, think that sundown on Friday evening is the beginning of the Sabbath.

CHAPTER 12

THE NEW TESTAMENT WRITERS AND THE SABBATH – PART 1

In this chapter, we come to one of the most contentious issues among Christians – the Sabbath. But in this book we are not interested in modern contentions regarding the Sabbath. We are just interested in the New Testament writers' view on the Sabbath. Did the New Testament writers observe the Sabbath? Furthermore, did they teach Gentile converts to observe the Sabbath? That is what we are concerned about in this chapter.

Now let's begin by recalling that all the writers of the New Testament were Jews. I brought this out in the very first chapter of this book. What day did Jews keep as the weekly holy day? The Sabbath. That is, they observed the weekly holy day on the seventh day of the Biblical week. So in Biblical time, they observed the Sabbath from sundown Friday to sundown Saturday. The Book of Acts records what the New Testament writers did in this regard. As we shall see, The Book of Acts consistently records that they kept the Sabbath as the weekly holy day. But did they teach the Gentiles to observe the first day of the week? We will answer this question as we go along.

There is only one mention of the Sabbath in the first twelve chapters of Acts. In Acts 1:12 we read: "Then they returned to Jerusalem from the mount called Olivet, which is near Jerusalem, a Sabbath day's journey away." A Sabbath day's journey was the distance which someone could walk on foot on the Sabbath day. At this point, the church consisted only of converted Jews. What did Jews do? They kept the Sabbath. Since they were all Sabbath keepers, this may be why there are no further mentions of the Sabbath in the first twelve chapters of The Book of Acts.

However, in The Book of Acts, Chapter 13, these Jewish believers in Christ began the first missionary journey to the Gentiles. The Lord had already shown them through the conversion of Cornelius and his household (recorded in Acts 10) that the Gentiles could be saved. But the missionary journey of Paul and Barnabas recorded in Acts 13 and 14 was the first concerted effort of the church to evangelize Gentiles. Consequently, if the holy day was to be changed from the seventh day of the week to the first day of the week for the Gentiles, we should find evidence of such a change in Paul's missionary journeys to the Gentiles.

After first going to the island of Cyprus, the New Testament records the arrival of Paul and Barnabas in Pisidian Antioch as follows: "But going on from Perga, they arrived at Pisidian Antioch, and on the Sabbath day they went into the synagogue and sat down." (Acts 13:14) In Chapter 4 of this book we showed that the New Testament writers went to the temple when in Jerusalem and to the synagogue when away from Jerusalem. In Chapter 5 we saw that there were three distinct groups in the synagogue – Jews, proselytes, and God-fearers. The Jews themselves considered the proselytes Jews, but the God-fearers they still considered Gentiles. Consequently, we demonstrated that when Paul and Barnabas went into any synagogue in the diaspora, they knew that they were reaching out to both Jews and Gentiles. That is, their evangelism targeted Jews and God-fearing Gentiles who already had some base in Biblical thinking through their involvement in the synagogue.

Next, let us note what happened after Paul finished his message in the synagogue. "As Paul and Barnabas were going out, the people kept begging that these things might be spoken to them the next Sabbath." (Act 13:42) Were these just Jews asking Paul and Barnabas to return the following Sabbath? The Acts 13 account continues: "Now when the meeting of the synagogue had broken up, many of the Jews and of the God-fearing proselytes followed Paul and Barnabas, who, speaking to them, were urging them to continue in the grace of God." (Acts 13:43) Two groups in the synagogue are mentioned here – "the Jews" and "the God-fearing proselytes." The proselytes and the God-fearers were two distinct groups in the synagogue, but here we find the designations mixed together. Although the expression "God-fearing proselytes" could refer to both proselytes and God-fearers, I choose to go with the noun here and believe that this was a reference only to Gentiles who had made a complete conversion to Judaism. The NIV translation bears this out as it translates "God-fearing proselytes" as "devout converts to Judaism." So clearly Paul reached both Jews and proselytes with his message at Pisidian Antioch. Did he also reach God-fearers?

"The next Sabbath nearly the whole city assembled to hear the word of the Lord." (Acts 13:44) Pisidian Antioch was a predominantly Gentile city in Asia Minor. Jews would have been only a small minority in Pisidian Antioch. So when "nearly the whole city" came together "to hear the word of the Lord," then Paul's audience was primarily Gentiles. To put this another way, on his first Sabbath in Pisidian Antioch, Paul preached primarily to Jews, but on his second Sabbath there he preached primarily to Gentiles. So let's not miss the obvious here: On his second Sabbath in Pisidian Antioch Paul preached the good news to Gentiles. He didn't tell those Gentiles to come back the next day on the first day of the week to hear the gospel. He went right ahead and preached to them on the Sabbath day. In Paul's first missionary journey the first gospel message clearly directed at Gentiles was preached on the Sabbath day.

Did Paul and Barnabas continue the pattern of going to the synagogue first on the remainder of their missionary journey? "In Iconium they entered the synagogue of the Jews together, and spoke in such a manner that a large number of people believed, both of Jews and of Greeks." (Acts 14:1) When did the synagogue meet? On the Sabbath. So although the Sabbath is not specifically mentioned in Acs 14:1, this is still a reference to the Sabbath since the synagogue met on the Sabbath. And who did Paul and Barnabas reach here? "A large number of people believed, both of Jews and of Greeks." Since this Scripture refers to Greeks in the synagogue, it is a clear reference to God-fearers. Both Jews and God-fearing Greeks accepted Christ through the preaching of the gospel at Iconium on the Sabbath.

After Paul and Barnabas completed the first missionary journey to the Gentiles, the Jerusalem council met to determine whether anyone had to get circumcised and keep the law of Moses in order to be saved. The council decided this question in the negative: no one had to get circumcised and keep the law of Moses in order to be saved. Then at the end of their discussion the council agreed on four conditions to which the Gentiles should adhere. However, the council did not declare that these behaviors were necessary for salvation. (That would have been contrary to the conclusion which they already reached – that salvation is by grace without any works of the law.) In the chapter on the Jerusalem council, we noted that there were two possibilities which could have explained the decision by the council. Either the council members agreed to this decision because they thought that failure to observe these behaviors could weaken the consciences of the Gentiles, resulting in them questioning their salvation. Or the council members agreed to this decision as a sop to James and the party of the circumcision, knowing that those who would deliver the letters laying out the recommended behaviors would go on preaching salvation by grace without the works of the law.

Some have argued that the decision by the Jerusalem council did away with the Sabbath for the Gentiles. All who so interpret the council's decision ignore three things. First, all the council members were Jews who kept the Sabbath. Second, Paul and Barnabas related the record of their missionary trip in Acts 15:12. We know from all the Scriptures which we covered earlier in this chapter that Paul and Barnabas not only kept the Sabbath on this trip, but also that they didn't teach the Gentiles that any other day of the week was the Sabbath. Third, at the Jerusalem council, James himself declared: "For Moses from ancient generations has in every city those who preach him, since he is read in the synagogues every Sabbath." (Acts 15:21) If the Sabbath were being done away with by the Jerusalem council, it would make no sense for James to make this statement. But he did. James knew that Paul and Barnabas were not only going to the synagogues, but also teaching the converted Gentiles to go to the synagogues. So James was confident that the converted Gentiles would continue to hear the law of Moses "in the synagogues every Sabbath."

In Acts 16:13 we find the next mention of the Sabbath in The Book of Acts: "And on the Sabbath day we went outside the gate to a riverside, where we were supposing that there would be a place of prayer; and we sat down and began speaking to the women who had assembled." Here Paul and Silas were in Philippi in Macedonia. Yet there is no mention of them going to the synagogue. Why? As I first noted in Chapter 5, there must not have been a synagogue in Philippi. So Paul and Silas went to a riverside outside the city where they "were supposing that there would be a place of prayer." Evidently, the Jews in the diaspora who lived in areas where there was no synagogue had the habit of assembling for prayer by riversides on the Sabbath. Why else would Paul and Silas suppose that there would be a place of prayer there? In addition, we also noted in Chapter 5 that Jews would be the people who assembled for prayer on the Sabbath. Sun-worshipping Greeks and Romans would not be doing this.

The other important thing that we want to note about this Scripture is what it doesn't say. Acts 16:13 does not say that Paul and Silas went out by a riverside on the first day of the week. If the Sabbath were replaced by the first day at the Jerusalem council, then they should have been out by the riverside on the first day of the week. But they were not. Instead, they continued the pattern of doing their primary evangelism on the Sabbath day.

"Now when they had traveled through Amphipolis and Apollonia, they came to Thessalonica, where there was a synagogue of the Jews. And according to Paul's custom, he went to them, and for three Sabbaths reasoned with them from the Scriptures." (Acts 17:1-2) What was Paul's custom? "For three Sabbaths" in succession Paul went to the synagogue. Paul's custom was to go to the synagogue on the Sabbath day. His custom was not to go to church on Sunday. How do we miss this? How do we read right over this? Paul's custom was to keep the Sabbath. Everything that Paul wrote in his letters needs to be interpreted in terms of the New Testament record that Paul was a Sabbath keeper.

In Acts 18 we find Paul in Corinth. "And he was reasoning in the synagogue every Sabbath and trying to persuade Jews and Greeks." (Acts 18:4) This is the second time in two chapters that the New Testament records Paul's habit of Sabbath observance. The Bible declares that the truth of any matter is established by two or three witnesses. (Matthew 18:16 and Deuteronomy 19:15) Acts 17:2 is one witness that Paul was a seventh-day Sabbath keeper and Acts 18:4 is another witness to the same truth. If you have believed that Paul was a Sunday keeper, correct your theology. The Scriptures give emphatic testimony that Paul was a Sabbath keeper.

Moreover, who was Paul trying to reach in the synagogue at Corinth? "Jews and Greeks." In other words, Paul was trying to reach Jews and God-fearing Greeks in the synagogue at Corinth. This is totally consistent with what Paul did throughout all his missionary journeys. The Book of Acts records what the New Testament writers actually did; what they actually did was observe the Sabbath day.

Plus, as we have seen in this study, Paul and his missionary helpers taught their converts to observe the Sabbath day. They didn't teach the God-fearing Greeks whom they reached in the synagogue to start meeting on Sunday. Rather, they taught them to continue meeting in the synagogue on the Sabbath day. There is no evidence that they taught other Gentile converts anything else. Eventually, we find Christians gathering in house meetings as well as attending synagogue meetings. But there is no evidence that those house meetings were either exclusively or predominantly on Sunday.

CHAPTER 13

THE NEW TESTAMENT WRITERS AND THE SABBATH – PART 2

In the previous chapter, we saw that throughout The Book of Acts, the 1st Century Jewish believers in Jesus Christ observed the seventh-day Sabbath as the weekly holy day. We also saw that they taught their Gentile converts to observe the Sabbath. The first Gentiles whom these Jewish believers reached with the gospel were God-fearing Gentiles who were already going to synagogue services every Sabbath. Then, as long as these Jewish believers were welcome in the synagogue, they continued to bring Gentile converts to the synagogue. The apostle James recognized this reality when he declared at the Jerusalem council: "For Moses from ancient generations has in every city those who preach him, since he is read in the synagogues every Sabbath." (Acs 15:21) Since the Jerusalem council was then sending a letter to the churches of the Gentiles, James' statement was a recognition of the fact that Paul and Barnabas were taking Gentile converts to the synagogue.

    The Book of Acts is the last historical book in the New Testament. After Acts there are only epistles and the prophetic book of Revelation. The epistles were written to the believers who found Christ in Acts. The Book of Acts gives the record of what the New Testament believers actually did. So the epistles cannot be interpreted contrary to the record in Acts unless they make direct statements showing that the New Testament writers did indeed change their beliefs. In this chapter we will examine what little the New Testament writers said about the Sabbath in their epistles.

The truth is that the New Testament writers said very little not only about the Sabbath, but also about the first four of the Ten Commandments. Why? Because the Ten Commandments were givens for all Jews. And that included all the Jews who became believers in Jesus Christ. As we saw earlier in this book, the New Testament writers had come to see that they neither got saved by keeping commandments nor stay saved by keeping commandments. Nevertheless, we also observed that they still believed that the Holy Spirit would lead them to keep the commandments. Since the Sabbath was one of the Ten Commandments, their belief in keeping the Ten Commandments would include the fourth commandment.

In Romans 14 we run into a passage that some interpret to do away with the Sabbath. The key verse in this regard is Romans 14:5: "One person regards one day above another, another regards every day alike. Each person must be fully persuaded in his own mind." The apostle Paul wrote Romans 14. As we have already observed, it was Paul's custom to keep the Sabbath. (See Acts 17:2 and Acts 18:4.) Paul believed that God Himself rested on the Sabbath day. (See Genesis 2:2-3.) Paul believed that God included the Sabbath day in the Ten Commandments. (See Exodus 20:8-11.) No 1st Century believer would have thought that Paul was talking about the Sabbath in Romans 14.

So what was Paul talking about in Romans 14? I believe that he was talking about national and local holidays. These would be holidays like Memorial Day and Labor Day in the United States. Or they would be holidays like Cinco de Mayo in most of Latin America. Rome had conquered many different nations and cultures, and these conquered peoples had their own national and local holidays. Should believers in Christ observe these days? Paul's advice was simple: If believers wanted to observe these days, that was okay. And if they didn't want to observe these days, that was okay as well. "Each person must be fully persuaded in his own mind."

The only detailed discussion of the Sabbath day in the letters is in Hebrews 4. Hebrews is a letter written by a Hebrew to a group of Hebrew believers. Or if you prefer, Hebrews is a letter written by a Jew to a group of Jewish believers. So the writer was a Sabbath keeper and his audience were all Sabbath keepers. The idea that a Jew writing to other Jews would be telling them that the Sabbath was done away with is an absurd idea. Let's review the passage to see what the writer wrote.

"Therefore, let us fear if, while a promise remains of entering His rest, any one of you may seem to come short of it. For indeed we have had good news preached to us, just as they also; but the word they heard did not profit them, because it was not united by faith in those who heard. For we who have believed enter that rest, just as He has said, 'AS I SWORE IN MY WRATH, THEY SHALL NOT ENTER MY REST,' although His works were finished from the foundation of the world. For He has said somewhere concerning the seventh day: 'AND GOD RESTED ON THE SEVENTH DAY FROM ALL HIS WORKS'; and again in this passage, 'THEY SHALL NOT ENTER MY REST.' Therefore, since it remains for some to enter it, and those who formerly had good news preached to them failed to enter because of disobedience,

He again fixed a certain day, 'TODAY,' saying in David after so long a time just as has been said before, 'TODAY IF YOU HEAR HIS VOICE, DO NOT HARDEN YOUR HEARTS.' For if Joshua had given them rest, He would not have spoken of another day after that. So there remains a Sabbah rest for the people of God." (Hebrews 4:1-9)

Remember the writer of this passage was a Sabbath keeper and his audience were all Sabbath keepers. Some today affirm that this passage teaches that the seventh-day Sabbath has been replaced by an eternal rest in the Spirit. No 1st Century Jewish believer in Christ would have interpreted this passage that way. What the writer to the Hebrews was teaching his fellow Hebrews was that the Sabbath had a spiritual meaning beyond being a day of physical rest. From the Sabbath, we should learn not only to rest physically on the seventh day, but also to rest spiritually just as "God rested on the seventh day from all His works." (Hebrews 4:4) Beyond the seventh-day Sabbath which they all observed, "there remains a Sabbath rest for the people of God." (Hebrews 4:9)

Finally, some have argued that the King James Version shows that the Sabbath was done away with here because it doesn't use the word "Sabbath" in Hebrews 4:9. "There remaineth therefore a rest to the people of God." (Hebrews 4:9 KJV) Looking up "rest" in Hebrews 4:9 in Young's Concordance, we find that the Greek word translated "rest" here is *sabbatismos*. The concordance also informs us that the literal meaning of *sabbatismos* is "a sabbath rest." So the King James translation of "rest" is insufficient. The New American Standard translation of

"Sabbath rest" is more accurate. Plus, the NAS translation completes the thought that the spiritual Sabbath rest is in addition to the physical Sabbath rest of the fourth commandment.

Finally, some affirm that the expression "the Lord's day" in Revelation 1:10 is a reference to Sunday. Throughout the rest of the Bible this expression is translated "the day of the Lord." In the Scriptures this expression consistently refers to the day of judgment - not to Sunday. (For the record, the word "Sunday" is never used in the Scriptures.) What does the book of Revelation prophesy about? The end of the world and the day of judgment. "The Lord's Day" refers to the day of judgment. It refers neither to Sunday nor the Sabbath day.

CHAPTER 14

TWO OTHER DIFFERENCES OF NOTE

In this chapter, we will take up two other differences between the 1st Century church and the church today. I don't believe that these differences are as important as the differences we have already covered because they don't receive as much emphasis in the New Testament, but the New Testament writers still saw these issues differently than we do today.

The first of these differences is the name of Jesus. I once heard a speaker say that Jesus never heard himself called Jesus when He was here on earth. That's because Jesus is an English transliteration of the original Aramaic Yeshua. There was no English language in the 1st Century, and even if there was a predecessor language to modern English, it was not spoken in Palestine. When Jesus was here on earth, He was known by His original Aramaic name Yeshua (or possibly by His original Hebrew name Yehoshua).

Yeshua was first transliterated into Greek, then later into Latin, and much later into English. Words typically go through some changes when they go through transliteration. The main reason for this is that some languages use letters that other languages do not use. Take the transliteration of the name of our Lord from the Aramaic Yeshua to the Greek *Iesous*. There is no "Y" in Greek. So they transliterated the Aramaic "Y" with the Greek "I." Similarly, there is no "SH" in Greek. So they transliterated the Aramaic "SH" with the Greek "S." So I believe that the original transliteration of Yeshua into Greek was *Iesua*. But the "A" is a feminine ending in Greek. So eventually they changed it to the masculine Greek ending "S."

Later the Greek "I" was transliterated into English as "J." This is a gross error in transliteration; there is no letter equivalent to the English "J" in Aramaic. The English letter "J' in no way represents the original sound of the Aramaic "Y." The least we should do in English today is to change Jesus to "Yesus" to eliminate a sound that was never there in our Lord's original name.

In the English-speaking world, God has saved many people in the name of Jesus. I believe that He has done so because Jesus is a sincere effort to transliterate the original Aramaic Yeshua. However, now that we know the truth about Yeshua, I believe that God would bless the church much more today if we used Yeshua instead of Jesus. Because most modern Christians have such an emotional attachment to saying Jesus, I believe that many would find saying Yeshua instead very difficult to do. But habits can be changed when people make up their minds to change them.

The other difference that I will take up in this chapter is the Biblical feasts of the Lord. The Biblical feasts are laid out in detail in Leviticus 23. In their order of occurrence in the Hebrew calendar, the feasts are Passover, Unleavened Bread, Firstfruits, Pentecost (Feast of Weeks), Trumpets, Day of Atonement, and Tabernacles (Including the Last Great Day). Because Firstfruits is part of the Feast of Unleavened Bread, I will not treat it as a separate feast here. All the feasts are celebrated on certain days of the year on the Hebrew calendar. Passover is on the 14th day of the first month,

Unleavened Bread on the 15th through the 21st days of the first month, Pentecost 50 days after the weekly Sabbath during Unleavened Bread, Trumpets on the 1st day of the seventh month, Day of Atonement on the 10th day of the seventh month, and Tabernacles on the 15th through the 22nd day of the seventh month (with the 22nd day being the Last Great Day). This is one of the reasons why we need to think in terms of God's calendar. All the Biblical feasts are set to God's calendar.

The New Testament record is very clear on the Biblical feasts. Jesus kept the feasts and all His disciples kept the feasts. Likewise, all the writers of the New Testament kept the feasts. References to Jesus observing Passover and Unleavened Bread include Luke 2:41-43, John 2:13, John 2:23, Matthew 26:17-19, Mark 14:12-16, Luke 22:1, Luke 22:8-16, and John 13:1. Jesus kept the Feast of Tabernacles in John 7:2-39. John 7:37 refers specifically to Jesus observing the Last Great Day of this feast. Although there are no specific mentions of Jesus keeping the other feasts, the is no reason to believe that He didn't keep them. Jesus was a Jew; the Jews observed all the feasts.

Does this pattern of feast observance continue in The Book of Acts? The answer is yes. "When the day of Pentecost had come, they were all together in one place." (Acts 2:1) Here we find the 120 disciples in Jerusalem observing the day of Pentecost. The account in Acts 2 goes on to tell us that the Holy Spirit fell on the 120 disciples and they then spoke in tongues and magnified God.

"When he (Herod) saw that it pleased the Jews, he proceeded to arrest Peter also. Now it was during the days of Unleavened Bread. When he had seized him, he put him in prison, delivering him to four squads of soldiers to guard him, intending after the Passover to bring him out before the people." (Acts 12:3-4) Here we find a reference to both the Feast of Unleavened Bread and the Passover (the day before Unleavened Bread). At that time both the Jews and the disciples of Jesus were observing these holy days. The account mentions the holy days as the time when Peter was imprisoned by Herod. If no one had been keeping Passover and Unleavened Bread, the references to these feasts would have been meaningless. (Note: The King James Version uses "Easter" instead of "Passover" in Acts 12:4. This is a mistranslation. The Greek word here is *pesach* and it means Passover. All modern English versions translate *pesach* as "Passover" in Acts 12:4.)

"And he (Paul) was accompanied by Sopater of Berea, the son of Pyrrhus, and by Aristarchus and Secundus of the Thessalonians, and Gaius of Derbe, and Timothy, and Tychicus and Trophimus of Asia. But these had gone on ahead and were waiting for us at Troas. We sailed from Philippi after the days of Unleavened Bread, and came to them at Troas within five days; and here we stayed seven days." (Acts 20:4-6) The reference to "the days of Unleavened Bread" at Philippi is a clear reference to the Feast of Unleavened Bread. Because Paul and those who were with him wanted to observe Unleavened Bread, they kept the feast first and then sailed from Philippi. A few have suggested that Paul just kept this feast at Philippi by himself. However, the use of the word "we" at the start of verse 6 indicates that Paul observed this feast with those who were with him. The truth is that all the feasts were commanded as group observances in the Bible. (A review of when God first gave the Biblical feasts in Leviticus 23 makes this clear.) No Jew would observe any Biblical feast alone.

"For Paul had decided to sail past Ephesus so that he would not have to spend time in Asia; for he was hurrying to be in Jerusalem, if possible, on the day of Pentecost." (Acts 20:16 NAS) Here Paul was trying to get to Jerusalem in time to observe Pentecost in Jerusalem. In this case he would have been observing Pentecost only with his fellow converted Jews. As we noted earlier, Gentiles were not allowed in the temple in Jerusalem. But from both Acts 20:4-6 and Acts 20:16 we can see that Paul was still keeping the Biblical feasts. If the feasts had been done away with, he would not be doing so.

Did the New Testament writers teach the Gentiles to observe the feasts? The Scripture passage in Acts 20:4-6 indicates that they did. But a more decisive Scripture is found in Paul's first epistle to the Corinthians. "Clean out the old leaven so that you may be a new lump, just as you are in fact unleavened. For Christ our Passover also has been sacrificed. Therefore let us celebrate the feast, not with old leaven, nor with the leaven of malice and wickedness, but with the unleavened bread of sincerity and truth." (I Corinthians 5:7-8 NAS) "Celebrate the feast" in verse 8 refers back to "Passover" in verse 7. The Corinthian congregation was a Christian congregation of both converted Jews and Gentiles. Since it was in Greece, the majority of the congregation was undoubtedly converted Gentiles. So in I Corinthians 5:7-8 Paul encouraged a congregation of primarily Gentile converts to keep the feast of Passover. The evidence is right here: the New Testament writers were teaching their Gentile converts to keep the Biblical feasts.

Finally, some have argued that Colossians 2:16-17 teaches that the feasts are done away with. Colossians was written by Paul. We have already seen that Paul kept the feasts (Acts 20:4-6 and Acts 20:16) and that he taught Gentile converts to keep the feasts (I Corinthians 5:7-8). So any interpretation of Colossians 2:16-17 which teaches that the feasts are done away with cannot be correct.

"Therefore no one is to act as your judge in regard to food or drink or in respect to a festival or a new moon or a Sabbath day – things which are a *mere* shadow of what is to come, but the substance belongs to Christ." (Colossians 2:16-17) In this case the New American Standard does not give the best translation of these verses. First, the translation "a Sabbath day" seems to imply that Paul was talking about the weekly Sabbath day in Colossians 2:16. He was not. The expression "a Sabbath day" refers back to the expression "a festival" (or feast). In this passage Paul was talking about the annual Sabbath days of the Biblical feasts – not about the weekly Sabbath day. Second, the word *"mere"* in verse 17 is in italics; that means that it was not in the original Greek text. The use of the word *"mere"* in the NAS just shows the prejudice of the translators of the NAS.

The King James Version gives a much better translation of Colossians 2:16-17. "Let no man therefore judge you in meat, or in drink, or in respect of a holyday, or of the new moon, or of the sabbath *days*: which are a shadow of things to come, but the body is of Christ." Holyday translates the Greek word *heorte*; it means festival or feast. So in the case of this word only the NAS gives a better translation. The word *"days"* is in italics because it is not in the original Greek. However, because "sabbath" in Colossians 2:16 refers back to "holyday" (feast) earlier in the verse, sabbath here refers to the annual holy days of the feasts – not to the weekly Sabbath day. So the word *"days"* just makes it clear that Paul is talking about the annual Sabbath days. Finally, Paul states that these annual Sabbath days "are a shadow of things to come, but the body is of Christ." The real substance of what the annual holy days mean is to be found in Christ. The fall feast days in particular are still shadowing things to come.

    What did Paul mean when he declared that the body (or substance) of the annual holy days is of Christ? Consider the spring feasts. Jesus Christ was crucified on Passover. Jesus Christ was raised from the dead during the Feast of Unleavened Bread. Jesus Christ poured out the Holy Spirit on Pentecost. Jesus showed us that He Himself is the substance of all the feasts. But He has yet to fulfill the fall feasts as He did the spring feasts. So the fall feasts remain "a shadow of things to come."

    All the New Testament writers kept the Biblical feasts. They didn't just keep them looking back to what God had done in the past. Rather, the New Testament writers observed the feasts looking ahead to what Jesus would do on the annual Sabbath days of the feasts in the future. We would do well to do likewise.

CHAPTER 15

JEWS, GENTILES, AND THE CHURCH

Today we don't think much about Jews and Gentiles (non-Jews). When we accept Jesus Christ as our Lord and Savior, we become part of His church. The body of Christ is His church and it includes every person who has accepted Jesus Christ as Lord and Savior. But the fact that both redeemed Jews and Gentiles are part of the church is not something that we typically think about as Gentiles who have put our faith in Jesus Christ. Today if a Jew believes in Jesus Christ, our view is that he has been added to the church.

Was it the view of the 1st Century church that if a Jew believed in Jesus Christ, he was added to the church? Yes and no. The answer was yes in the sense that every person who accepted Jesus Christ as his Lord and Savior became part of the church. Yet the answer was no in the sense that the 1st Century church viewed converted Jews as the natural members of the church and converted Gentiles as the unnatural members of the church who were grafted in contrary to nature. This view may sound strange to us today, but we need to recognize two things in this regard. First, all the original members of the church were converted Jews. Second, all the writers of the New Testament were converted Jews. One reason that we go off track in our thinking today is that we have a Gentile worldview of the church – not the original Jewish worldview of the church.

Consider the words of Jesus in the matter of Jews and Gentiles. Speaking to the Samaritan woman at the well, Jesus said: "You worship what you do not know; we worship what we know, for salvation is of the Jews." (John 4:22) "Salvation is of the Jews." These are the words of Jesus Christ. Jesus did not say that salvation is of the Gentiles or even of the church. This is not complicated: Jesus is our salvation and Jesus was a Jew. As we shall see, the New Testament writers all took the approach that "salvation is of the Jews."

Paul takes up the matter of Jews and Gentiles and how salvation came to the Gentiles in Romans 11. He commences his discussion as follows: "I say then, God has not rejected His people, has He? May it never be! For I too am an Israelite, a descendant of Abraham, of the tribe of Benjamin. God has not rejected His people whom He foreknew. Or do you not know what the Scripture says in the passage about Elijah, how he pleads with God against Israel? 'Lord, THEY HAVE KILLED YOUR PROPHETS, THEY HAVE TORN DOWN YOUR ALTARS, AND I ALONE AM LEFT, AND THEY ARE SEEKING MY LIFE.' But what is the divine response to him? 'I HAVE KEPT FOR MYSELF SEVEN THOUSAND MEN WHO HAVE NOT BOWED THE KNEE TO BAAL.' In the same way then, there has also come to be a remnant according to God's gracious choice." (Romans 11:1-5) These Scriptures address one of the errant teachings prevalent in much of the church today – that is, that the church has replaced Israel. "God has not rejected His people whom He foreknew." If God has not rejected Israel, then the church has not replaced Israel. As we continue in Romans 11, we will see that God has provided the church in addition to Israel – not as a replacement for Israel. There is always "a remnant" of Israel "according to God's gracious choice."

Continuing his discussion, Paul speaks of Jews and Gentiles further: "I say then, they (the Jews) did not stumble so as to fall, did they? May it never be! But by their transgression salvation has come to the Gentiles, to make them jealous. Now if their transgression is riches for the world and their failure is riches for the Gentiles, how much more will their fulfillment be! But I am speaking to you who are Gentiles. Inasmuch then as I am an apostle of Gentiles, I magnify my ministry, if somehow I might move to jealousy my fellow countrymen and save some of them. For if their rejection is the reconciliation of the world, what will their acceptance be but life from the dead?" (Romans 11:11-15)

How did salvation come to the Gentiles? By the transgression of the Jews. In other words, if the Jews had not sinned and rejected Jesus in the 1st Century, salvation would not have come to the Gentiles at that time. "Their failure is the riches for the Gentiles." Furthermore, "if their rejection is the reconciliation of the world, what will their acceptance be but life from the dead?" The salvation of all Israel is such an important matter in God's plan that when it happens, it will be "life from the dead" forever.

Paul continues by addressing the Gentile believers as follows: "But if some of the branches were broken off, and you, being a wild olive, were grafted in among them and became partaker with them of the rich root of the olive tree, do not be arrogant toward the branches; but if you are arrogant, remember that it is not you who supports the root, but the root supports you. You will say then, 'Branches were broken off so that I might be grafted in.' Quite right, they were broken off for their unbelief, but you stand by your faith. Do not be conceited, but fear;

for if God did not spare the natural branches, He will not spare you either. Behold then the kindness and severity of God; to those who fell, severity, but to you, God's kindness, if you continue in His kindness; otherwise you also will be cut off. And they also, if they do not continue in their unbelief, will be grafted in, for God is able to graft them in again. For if you were cut off from what is by nature a wild olive tree, and were grafted contrary to nature into a cultivated olive tree, how much more will these who are the natural branches be grafted into their own olive tree?" (Romans 11:17-24)

     Basically, in this passage Paul makes an analogy between the church and an olive tree. The Jews are the natural branches that grow with the olive tree. The Gentiles, in contrast, are the unnatural branches that are grafted into the olive tree. God's olive tree had nothing but Jewish branches originally. But when most 1st Century Jews rejected Jesus Christ as their Lord and Savior, God grafted Gentile branches into His olive tree. In consequence, Gentile believers in Christ should "not be arrogant" toward Jewish believers. We Gentiles only got into God's olive tree because of "God's kindness."

     Paul concludes his thoughts on Jews and Gentiles as follows: "For I do not want you, brethren, to be uninformed of this mystery – so that you will not be wise in your own estimation – that a partial hardening has happened to Israel until the fulness of the Gentiles has come in; and so all Israel will be saved; just as it is written, 'THE DELIVERER WILL COME FROM ZION, HE WILL REMOVE UNGODLINESS FROM JACOB.' 'THIS IS MY COVENANT WITH THEM, WHEN I TAKE THEIR SINS AWAY.'" (Romans 11:25-27) Because of the "partial hardening" of Israel, we now live in an age when salvation is offered to the Gentiles. But when "the fulness of the Gentiles has come in," this age will come to an end. Then "all Israel will be saved." Since Paul has distinguished Jews from Gentiles throughout this passage, he is talking about Jews when he declares that "all Israel will be saved." The idea that the church has replaced Israel is an "arrogant" Gentile idea. There is no way that you can reconcile false replacement theology with the truth that the church consists of natural branch Jews and grafted-in branch Gentiles.

Is the Romans 11 view of Jews, Gentiles, and the church sustained throughout the New Testament? Consider these words of Paul in his Epistle to the Ephesians: "Therefore remember that formerly you, the Gentiles in the flesh, who are called 'Uncircumcision' by the so-called 'Circumcision,' which is performed in our flesh by human hands – remember that you were at that time separate from Christ, excluded from the commonwealth of Israel, and strangers to the covenants of promise, having no hope and without God in the world. But now in Christ Jesus you who formerly were far off have been brought near by the blood of Christ." (Ephesians 2:11-13) Without Christ the Gentiles were "excluded from the commonwealth of Israel." The picture is the same here as in Romans 11; the church ("the commonwealth of Israel") started with natural branch Jews and then grafted-in Gentiles were added to it.

Although Peter does not mention Jews and Gentiles specifically in his epistles, he does make the following statement: "For this is contained in Scripture: 'BEHOLD, I LAY IN ZION A CHIEF CORNER STONE, A PRECIOUS CORNER stone, AND HE WHO BELIEVES IN HIM WILL NOT BE DISAPPOINTED.'"

(I Peter 2:6) Where is Zion? Zion is the holy mountain where the temple was built in Jerusalem. Although Zion in a secondary meaning can be spiritualized and refer to the church, in its primary meaning Zion always refers to Israel. Jesus was the "choice stone" laid in Zion. He was the Jew sent first for the salvation of Jews. Then after His resurrection, He extended His salvation to Gentiles as well. So In I Peter 2:9 we read: "But you are A CHOSEN RACE, A royal PRIESTHOOD, A HOLY NATION, A PEOPLE FOR GOD'S OWN POSSESSION, so that you may proclaim the excellencies of Him who has called you out of darkness into His marvelous light." All the words in capital letters in this Scripture are quotes from the Old Testament. In other words, "A CHOSEN RACE," A HOLY NATION," and "A PEOPLE FOR GOD'S OWN POSSESSION" are all appellations originally applied to Israel. So Peter is saying that because of God's grace these appellations now refer to the church as well. Peter's picture of the church is the same as Paul's: the church consists of Jews first with Gentiles added in.

"For I am not ashamed of the gospel, for it is the power of God for salvation to everyone who believes, to the Jews first and also to the Greek." (Romans 1:16) Salvation is to the Jew first and also to the Gentile ("the Greek"). Together all saved Jews and Gentiles make up Christ's church.

CHAPTER 16

WHAT THE NEW TESTAMENT WRITERS EMPHASIZED – PART 1

In this book, we have focused primarily on how the New Testament writers saw things differently than do Bible-believing Christians today. However, on the most important issues, they saw things quite similarly to the way that Bible-believing Christians do today. As we will see in the next two chapters, the Bible-believing church today sees the most important issues pretty much the same as did the New Testament writers.

The number one issue that the New Testament writers emphasized was Jesus and His salvation. Consider just a few verses in this regard. "She (Mary) will bear a Son, and you shall call His name Jesus, for He will save His people from their sins." (Matthew 1:21) "For today in the city of David there has been born for you a Savior, who is Christ the Lord." (Luke 2:11) "Let it be known to all of you and to all the people of Israel, that by the name of Jesus Christ the Nazarene, whom you crucified, whom God raised from the dead – by this name this man stands before you in good health. He is the STONE WHICH WAS REJECTED BY YOU, THE BUILDERS, but WHICH BECAME THE CHIEF CORNER stone. And there is salvation in no one else; for there is no other name under heaven that has been given among men by which we must be saved." (Acts 4:10-12) "For I determined to know nothing among you except Jesus Christ, and Him crucified." (I Corinthians 2:2) "We have seen and testify that the Father has sent the Son to be the Savior of the world." (I John 4:14)

There are many other Scriptures which I could quote regarding Jesus Christ and His salvation. However, the above list is sufficient to get the point. The emphasis of the New Testament writers was Jesus, Jesus, Jesus. The emphasis was that Jesus is Savior, Jesus is Christ, and Jesus is Lord. In the above paragraph, I quoted a number of Scriptures showing that Jesus is Savior. "Therefore let all the house of Israel know for certain that God has made Him both Lord and Christ – this Jesus whom you crucified." (Acts 2:36) Jesus isn't just Savior; Jesus is both Lord and Christ. "For this reason also, God highly exalted Him, and bestowed on Him the name which is above every name, so that at the name of Jesus EVERY KNEE WILL BOW, of those who are in heaven and on earth and under the earth, and that every tongue will confess that Jesus Christ is Lord, to the glory of God the Father." (Philippians 2:9-11) Again there are many other Scriptures which I could quote on the subject of Jesus being both Lord and Christ, but the Scriptures just quoted are sufficient to bring this truth across.

The New Testament writers also emphasized the death, burial, and resurrection of our Lord Jesus Christ. Moreover, they emphasized His crucifixion death. In this regard consider the following Scriptures: "Men of Israel, listen to these words: Jesus the Nazarene, a man attested to you by God with miracles and wonders and signs which God performed through Him in your midst, just as you yourselves know – this Man, delivered over by the predetermined plan and foreknowledge of God, you nailed to a cross by the hands of godless men and put Him to death. But God raised Him up again, putting an end to the agony of death, since it was impossible for Him to be held in its power." (Acts 2:22-24) "For those who live in Jerusalem, and their rulers, recognizing neither Him (Jesus) nor the utterances of the prophets which are read every Sabbath, fulfilled these by condemning Him. And though they found no ground for putting Him to death, they asked Pilate that He be executed. When they had carried out all that was written concerning Him, they took Him down from the cross and laid Him in a tomb. But God raised Him from the dead." (Acts 13:27-30) "Or do you not know that all of us who have been baptized into Christ have been baptized into His death? Therefore we have been buried with Him through baptism into death, so that as Christ was raised from the dead through the glory of the Father, so we too might walk in newness of life." (Romans 6:3-4) "For I determined to know nothing among you except Jesus Christ, and Him crucified." (I Corinthians 2:2) Again the Scriptures quoted here are just a few of many in the New Testament which emphasize the death, burial, and resurrection of Jesus Christ.

The New Testament writers also emphasized certain doctrinal truths. They did so not so much for doctrinal correctness, but much more for truths to be lived out as the Christian way of life. One of the most important of these doctrinal truths was grace. The New Testament Chistian Jews had to emphasize grace because the unbelieving Jews didn't see grace at all. The unbelieving Jews were trying hard to work their way to salvation. So the New Testament Christian Jews emphasized grace to get Christians to understand that their salvation was the gift of God without any works at all.

Regarding the grace of our Lord Jesus Christ, consider the following Scriptures: "Being justified as a gift by His grace through the redemption which is in Christ Jesus." (Romans 3:24) "For by grace you have been saved through faith; and that not of yourselves, it is the gift of God; not as a result of works, so that no one may boast." (Ephesians 2:8-9) "For the grace of God that bringeth salvation hath appeared to all men." (Titus 2:11 KJV) "You have been severed from Christ, you who are seeking to be justified by Law; you have fallen from grace." (Galatians 5:4) The New Testament writers were emphatic on this point: we are saved by grace without any works of the law. (We noted this truth before in the chapter on The New Testament Writers' Overall View of the Law.)

Moreover, since the New Testament writers emphasized grace, they emphasized the faith that grace produced. Look again at Ephesians 2:8-9: "For by grace you have been saved through faith; and that not of yourselves, it is the gift of God; not as a result of works, so that no one may boast." How important was faith to the New Testament writers? "And without faith it is impossible to please Him, for he who comes to God must believe that He is and that He is a rewarder of those who seek Him." (Hebrews 11:6) "For we walk by faith, not by sight." (II Corinthians 5:7) "For whatever is born of God overcomes the world; and this is the victory that has overcome the world – our faith." (I John 5:4) Faith was critically important to the New Testament writers because they all lived by faith.

CHAPTER 17

WHAT THE NEW TESTAMENT WRITERS EMPHASIZED – PART 2

What else did the New Testament writers emphasize? They gave some emphasis to many important truths. In particular, the New Testament writers emphasized love, the leading of the Holy Spirit, and the second coming of Jesus Christ. I will take up all three of these truths in this chapter.

The New Testament writers emphasized the love that God showed to us through the death of His Son Jesus Christ on the cross. There are many verses on this subject; I will quote just two. "But God demonstrates His own love toward us, in that while we were yet sinners, Christ died for us." (Romans 5:8) "In this is love, not that we loved God, but that He loved us and sent His Son to be the propitiation for our sins." (I John 4:10) However, we will devote more time here to the love that we are supposed to demonstrate ourselves.

The New Testament writers emphasized the love of Christians in two ways – loving God and loving others. Moreover, they had specific concepts of what it meant to love God and to love others. I will take up loving God first. Consider the following verses: "One of them, a lawyer, asked Him a question, testing Him, 'Teacher, which is the greatest commandment in the Law?' And He said to him, 'YOU SHALL LOVE THE LORD YOUR GOD WITH ALL YOUR HEART, AND WITH ALL YOUR SOUL, AND WITH ALL YOUR MIND. This is the first and foremost commandment.'"(Matthew 22:35-

38) "If you love Me, you will keep My commandments." (John 14:15) "He who has My commandments and keeps them is the one who loves Me; and he who loves Me will be loved by My Father, and I will love him and disclose Myself to him." (John 14:21) "For this is the love of God, that we keep His commandments, and His commandments are not burdensome." (I John 5:3)

From the above verses we are supposed to love God with all our emotion (our heart), all our will (our soul), and all our mental capacity (our mind). How do we do that? By keeping the commandments of Jesus (John 14:15) and the commandments of God (I John 5:3). Jesus gave His commandments in the Sermon on the Mount. God gave His Ten Commandments at Mount Sinai. I am sure that the verses quoted refer to more than just the commandments that Jesus gave in the Sermon on the Mount and the commandments that God gave at Mount Sinai. But these commandments are a good place to start.

Let's take just the first four of the Ten Commandments. They all relate to our relationship with God. How do we show God that we love Him? By not having any other gods before Him, by not making any idols, by not taking His name in vain, and by keeping the Sabbath day holy. When we keep these commandments by showing respect for God's Word, we show God that love Him.

Now let's return to Mathew 22. After answering the lawyer's question, Jesus continued: "The second is like it, 'YOU SHALL LOVE YOUR NEIGHBOR AS YOURSELF.' On these two commandments depend the whole Law and the Prophets." (Matthew 22:39-40) Considering the whole passage in Matthew 22:35-40, the Lord's complete answer to the lawyer's question was to love God first and to love our neighbor second. Look at the following verses regarding loving others: "Peace be to the brethren, and love with faith, from God the Father and the Lord Jesus Christ." (Ephesians 6:23) "Having so fond an affection for you, we were well-pleased to impart to you not the gospel of God only, but also our own lives, because you had become very dear to us." (I Thessalonian 2:8) "If someone says, 'I love God,' and hates his brother, he is a liar; for the one who does not love his brother whom he has seen, cannot love God whom he has not seen. And this commandment we have from Him, that the one who loves God should love his brother also." (I John 4:20-21) The New Testament writers put a strong emphasis on loving others.

How did the New Testament writers teach that we should show love to others? They taught how to show love in more than one way. But primarily they taught that we should show love to others by forgiving them and by meeting their physical needs. First, let's look at two Scriptures in which they taught forgiveness: "Be kind to one another, tenderhearted, forgiving each other, just as God in Christ also has forgiven you." (Ephesians 4:32) "Bearing with one another, and forgiving each other, whoever has a complaint against anyone, just as the Lord forgave you, so also should you." (Colossians 3:13)

Second, the New Testament writers taught showing love to others through meeting their physical needs. Again, let's look at two Scriptures: "Pure and undefiled religion in the sight of our God and Father is this: to visit orphans and widows in their distress, and to keep oneself unstained by the world." (James 1:27) "But whoever has the world's goods, and sees his brother in need and closes his heart against him, how does the love of God abide in him? Little children, let us not love with word or with tongue, but in deed and truth." (I John 3:17-18)

The New Testament writers also emphasized the leading of the Holy Spirit. In Acts 2:1-11 the Holy Spirit fell on the disciples in Jerusalem and the age of the Holy Spirit began. In Acts 4:24-30 we find the church in Jerusalem praying in unison under the anointing of the Holy Spirit. "And when they had prayed, the place where they had gathered together was shaken, and they were all filled with the Holy Spirit and began to speak the word of God with boldness." (Acts 4:31) The work of the Holy Spirit did not stop with the outpouring of the Holy Spirit on the day of Pentecost; it continued right on. Later In Acts we find five of the leaders of the church in Antioch praying and fasting to the Lord. (Acts 13:1) "While they were ministering to the Lord and fasting, the Holy Spirit said, 'Set apart for me Barnabas and Saul for the work to which I have called them.'" (Acts 13:2) Here the Holy Spirit set apart Barnabas and Saul for the first missionary journey to the Gentiles – a mission trip that changed world history.

In Acts 16 the Holy Spirit directed Paul and Silas not to speak the Word in Asia or Bithynia (at that time). Instead, He led them to go to Macedonia. (See Acts 16:6-10.) I could give other examples; suffice it to say that Acts is all about the leading of the Holy Spirit. Paul summarized the importance of the leading of the Holy Spirit with this statement: "For all who are being led by the Spirit of God, these are sons of God." (Romans 8:14) Moreover, in I Corinthians 2:10-12 Paul emphasized the role of the Holy Spirit in leading us into the revelation of the things of God. "For to us God revealed them through the Spirit; for the Spirit searches all things, even the depths of God. For who among men knows the thoughts of a man except the spirit of the man which is in him? Even so the thoughts of God no one knows except the Spirit of God. Now we have received, not the spirit of the world, but the Spirit who is from God, so that we may know the things freely given to us to us by God." Basically, the New Testament writers took the view that they didn't want to do anything without the leading of the Holy Spirit.

Finally, the New Testament writers emphasized the second coming of Jesus Christ. Jesus will not remain in heaven forever; eventually, He will return to rule the earth. Matthew records our Lord's own words regarding His return: "And then the sign of the Son of Man will appear in the sky, and then all the tribes of the earth will mourn, and they will see the SON OF MAN COMING ON THE CLOUDS OF THE SKY with power and great glory. And He will send forth His angels with A GREAT TRUMPET and THEY WILL GATHER TOGETHER His elect from the four winds, from one end of the sky to the other." (Matthew24:30-31) Paul records the second coming of Christ in these words: "For the Lord Himself will descend from heaven with a shout, with the voice of the archangel and with the trumpet of God, and the dead in Christ will rise first. Then we who are alive and remain will be caught up together with them in the clouds to meet the Lord in the air, and so we shall always be with the Lord." (I Thessalonians 4:16-17) The truth is that the book of Revelation is devoted to the second coming of Jesus Christ and the events that precede His return.

Considering the number of things that Jesus predicted in Matthew 24 that are now coming to pass in this world, we need to take seriously the Scriptures that warn us to be on the watch for His return. Jesus is coming back. The New Testament writers emphasized His return and we should do likewise today.

CHAPTER 18

HOUSE CHURCHES IN THE NEW TESTAMENT

Earlier in this book I mentioned that there were two places where Christians assembled to meet during the 1st Century A.D. They met in synagogues and they met in house churches. (Recall that 1st Century Jewish Christians also went to the temple in Jerusalem, but Gentile Christians were not allowed in the temple.) We extensively covered 1st Century Christians meeting in synagogues earlier in this book. In this chapter we will cover 1st Century Christians assembling in house churches.

House churches were part of 1st Century Christianity right from its inception. "Day by day continuing with one mind in the temple, and breaking bread from house to house, they were taking their meals together with gladness and sincerity of heart." (Acts 2:46) Immediately after the church was formed on the Day of Pentecost, we find Christians meeting "from house to house." Yes, they were eating together, but they were also learning the Scriptures, fellowshipping, and praying together. "They were continually devoting themselves to the apostles' teaching and to fellowship, to the breaking of bread and to prayer." (Acts 2:42)

Think this through: 1st Century Jewish Christians in Jerusalem could learn the basics of the Scriptures in the temple, but they could only get the Jewish point of view there. However, "the apostles' teaching" was the Christian point of view. The writers of the New

Testament were those apostles and they could only teach what Jesus Christ had revealed to them outside the temple. So the apostles taught "the apostles' teaching" in house churches.

Did the apostles and their followers try to teach Jesus Christ in the temple? Yes, they did. "And every day, in the temple and from house to house, they kept right on teaching and preaching Jesus as the Christ." (Acts 5:42) However, the unbelieving Jews who led the temple worship did not allow the Christians Jews to teach in the temple very long. Probably the last Christian message in the temple was Stephen's defense in Acts 7. After that we learn that "a great persecution began against the church in Jerusalem, and they were all scattered throughout the regions of Judea and Samaria, except the apostles." (Acts 8:1b) With this great persecution against Christian Jews, the unbelieving Jews no longer wanted them in the temple. Yet we see from Acts 5:42 that they continued meeting "from house to house." For the rest of the 1st Century the house church was the chief meeting place of the Christian church.

As we noted earlier in this book, when Paul and Barnabas took the gospel to the Gentiles, in every city they began their mission by reaching out to Jews and Gentiles in synagogues. Yet because Paul and Barnabas were often not received by the majority of the Jews in the synagogues, house churches were started in the diaspora right away. 1st Century Christians had to meet somewhere; if the local synagogue would not receive them, then the houses of different believers became the place of assembly for these early Christians. In the next few paragraphs we will look at some different house churches noted in the New Testament.

"Greet Prisca and Aquila, my fellow workers in Christ Jesus, who for my life risked their own necks, to whom not only I give thanks, but also all the churches of the Gentiles; also greet the church that is their house. Greet Epaenetus, my beloved, who is the first convert to Christ from Asia." (Romans 16:3-5) Prisca (Priscilla in the KJV) and Aquila had a church in their house. This does not mean that they had a church building inside their house. This means that some of the local believers met as a church in their house. Prisca and Aquila first appeared in the Scriptures in Acts 18 when they met Paul at Corinth. Acts 18:2 informs us that this couple came to Corinth from Italy. Romans 16:3-5 shows us that they returned to Italy and organized a church in their house in Rome.

The house church of Aquila and Prisca is referred to again in I Corinthians 16:19: "The churches of Asia greet you. Aquila and Prisca greet you heartily in the Lord, with the church that is in their house." Obviously the house church led by Aquila and Prisca was of some note for it to be mentioned twice in the New Testament. Undoubtedly "the churches of Asia" mentioned in this verse also referred to a group of house churches as we have no record of any New Testament church meeting anywhere other than in a synagogue or a house.

"Greet the brethren who are in Laodicea and also Nymphas and the church that is in her house." (Colossians 4:15) Here we find a church in Laodicea meeting in a house of a lady named Nymphas. As Paul did not suffer women to teach (see I Timothy 2:12), Nymphas was not the leader of this house church. Nevertheless, some or all of the believers in Laodicea met in her house. My guess is

The New Testament Writer's Worldview

that her house was either at a central location or that it was large enough to accommodate a group of believers.

"Paul, a prisoner of Christ Jesus, and Timothy our brother, to Philemon, our beloved brother and fellow worker, and to Apphia our sister, and to Archippus our fellow soldier, and to the church in your house." (Philemon 1-2) Philemon, the man to whom Paul addressed this letter, had a church meeting in his house. This is not a surprise. Paul wrote Philemon asking him to free his slave Onesimus who was working with Paul to spread the gospel. Since Philemon was well off enough to own slaves, his house would have been larger than the average Roman citizen's house. (Most Roman citizens were not well off enough to own slaves.) In this case, I believe that a local group of believers met in Philemon's house because it was in all likelihood the largest house of anybody in the church.

Although we do not find other house churches in the New Testament mentioned specifically by name, the New Testament epistles were primarily written to collections of house churches. For example, since the church in the house of Aquila and Prisca was in Roma, the epistle to the Romans was an epistle to all the house churches in Rome. The letter would be read in one house church in Rome and then passed on to another house church in Rome. Rome was too large a city to have only one house church. The letter to the Romans was undoubtedly sent to all the house churches in Rome. The same would have been true of the Epistle to the Ephesians. Ephesus was one of the largest cities in Asia Minor in the 1st Century AD. Like Rome, it was too large a city to have only one house church. The Epistle to the

Ephesians was undoubtedly sent to all the house churches in Ephesus.

Now the question arises: Did the 1st Century Christians have separate church buildings as we do today? We do not know for certain whether they did or not, but the answer is probably not. Since the Jews built their own synagogues, why didn't the 1st Century Jewish Christians build their own churches? I believe that there are three reasons why they did not, and I will take up all three.

First, the 1st Century Jewish Christians considered the synagogue as a place for the church to meet. Since most major cities in the Roman Empire had a synagogue, the early Jewish Christians attended the synagogue as a place of Christian worship. We have certainly shown in this book that the synagogue was where they went until the Jews excommunicated them in 70 A.D. The early Christians used the house church to teach specifically Christian doctrine. Otherwise, they met at the local synagogue.

Second, the 1st Century Christians preached against the pantheon of gods worshipped by the Romans (and the Greeks as well). Their strong stance for monotheism did not endear them to their polytheistic neighbors. To erect a building and call it a Christian church would have provoked the wrath of the Roman citizenry. Consider the riot at Ephesus recorded in Acts 19 when the heathen Greeks felt that their false goddess was under threat. (See Acts 19:23-34.) Can you imagine how bad the riot would have been if the Christians in Ephesus had attempted to erect a church building?

Third, most of the 1st Century Christians were poor. A rich man like Philemon was the exception. Most of them were poor and many were slaves like Onesimus.

Slaves typically didn't own anything other than their own clothes; slaves would not have possessed the funds to pay for erecting church buildings. Likewise, poor Roman citizens, although free, would not have possessed such funds either. The early church lacked the financial capability to erect church buildings.

Why is the matter of house churches important today? Since almost all churches now meet in separate church buildings, why should we take any interest in house churches? First, the view that almost all churches meet in separate church buildings now is our Western view of the world. Christians have no place to meet in many countries except in houses or fields. In other countries, although separate church buildings are tolerated, Christians can meet in these buildings, but they are not allowed to evangelize and they are often spied upon.

We will take a few examples. If you are a Christian in North Korea or Iran today, you cannot legally meet anywhere. Churches are not allowed in either country; so church buildings are certainly not allowed. In North Korea, you will be sent to a concentration camp just for possessing a Bible. You will certainly be sent there for any sort of Christian meeting in your house or anywhere else. Likewise, in Iran you will suffer a fine at the least or a prison sentence or even execution at the worst if you are caught participating in any sort of Christian meeting. In these countries, if you are a Christian and you want to meet with other Christians, you can only do so by meeting secretly with other Christians in houses or in fields.

If you are a Christian in China, the state does allow churches. However, if you meet in a church building, the state sends spies into your meetings to make sure that you are not being "too Christian." If the state determines that you are too Christian, they close down your church at the least or send you off to prison at the worst. Dedicated Christians in China have opted out of the government system; they meet secretly in houses. Of course, if these Christians are caught, the government sends them to a prison or a concentration camp.

Finally, in many Muslim countries, Christian churches are outwardly tolerated. In these countries, Christians are allowed to have church buildings and to meet in them. However, they are not allowed to evangelize Muslims or say anything against Allah or Muhammed. Muslims often beat or otherwise physically abuse Christians who evangelize other Muslims. Saying anything against Allah or Muhammed is considered blasphemy; it is usually punishable by death. Even in these outwardly tolerant nations house churches often become the best option for Bible-believing Christians.

In 2020 COVID arrived in America. Local governments in many states closed churches or limited the number of people who could assemble in them. (Of course, all of these state government orders were in violation of the First Amendment.) In some cases Christians who defied these state orders were arrested. Those who were arrested typically served little or no jail time. But we need to learn our lesson from this government overreach. Religious tolerance does not exist in America as it once did. Who knows what our government will do the next time there is some "COVID-like" threat? Who even knows what they will consider a threat next time? The day may soon come when house churches will be our best option. In fact, the day may come when house churches will be our only option.

CHAPTER 19

WHICH COMMANDMENTS DID THE NEW TESTAMENT WRITERS KEEP?

Which commandments did the New Testament writers keep? This is the most difficult question I ask in this book. The truth is that I don't have a definitive answer to this question. However, the New Testament writers tell me plenty about what they believed in regard to which commandments they kept. So I believe that my answer to this question is at least close to what they believed.

Earlier in this book we established that the New Testament writers kept the commandments of God. But which commandment did they keep? On the one hand, there are believers who affirm that the law is done away with. Although none of these believers affirm that the 1st Century church didn't observe any commandments, they still throw out all the commandments which they don't feel are necessary. On the other hand, there are believers who affirm that we should keep all the commandments in the law. However, some of the commandments in the law may be statutes and some of them may be judgments. The Pharisees became quite legalistic over the keeping of the commandments, but then they also added commandments which the Lord didn't give. We don't want to make the same mistake.

I will start with this question: Did the New Testament writers view all the commandments of equal weight? The answer is no. Jesus declared: "Whoever then annuls one of the least of these commandments, and teaches others to do the same, shall be called least in the kingdom of heaven; but whoever keeps and teaches them, he shall be called great in the kingdom of heaven." (Matthew 5:19) Jesus Himself used the expression "the least of these commandments." In other words, some commandments are of lesser importance than other commandments. Plus, Jesus stated that believers who do away with lesser commandments "shall be called least in the kingdom of heaven." As noted earlier in this book, commandment keeping has nothing to do with making it to heaven.

Again, when Jesus was asked, "Teacher, which is the greatest commandment in the Law?" (Matthew 22:36), He didn't reply that all the commandments are of equal weight. Instead, Jesus answered as follows: "And He said to him, 'YOU SHALL LOVE THE LORD YOUR GOD WITH ALL YOUR HEART, AND WITH ALL YOUR SOUL, AND WITH ALL YOUR MIND.' This is the greatest and foremost commandment. The second is like it, 'YOU SHALL LOVE YOUR NEIGHBOR AS YOURSELF.' On these two commandments depend the whole Law and the Prophets." (Matthew 22:37-40) Jesus clearly stated that there was a commandment of first importance and another of second importance. The idea that all commandments are of equal weight is not a Biblical concept. According to our Lord's own words, some commandments are of greater importance than others.

Now think about the two most important commandments stated by Jesus Himself. How do I show my love to God? When I don't put any gods before the LORD, when I don't erect any idols in my house, when I don't take the LORD's name in vain, and when I keep the

Sabbath day holy, I show God that I love Him. When I keep the first four of the Ten Commandments, I show God that I love Him. Loving God with all my heart, soul, and mind is not limited to keeping the first four of the Ten Commandments, but this is a good place to start. Similarly, how do I show my love to others? When I honor my father and my mother, when I don't murder, when I don't commit adultery, when I don't steal, when I don't lie, and when I don't covet anything that is not mine, I show love to others. When I keep the last six of the Ten Commandments, I show love to others. Loving others as myself is not limited to keeping the last six of the Ten Commandments, but this is a good place to start.

The truth is that both Jesus and Paul reinforced the Ten Commandments. When the rich young ruler asked Jesus what he needed to do to inherit eternal life, Jesus replied, "You know the commandments, 'DO NOT COMMIT ADULTERY, DO NOT MURDER, DO NOT STEAL, DO NOT BEAR FALSE WITNESS, HONOR YOUR FATHER AND MOTHER.'" (Luke 18:20) In His reply Jesus cited five of the Ten Commandments. Likewise, Paul wrote: "Owe nothing to anyone except to love one another; for he who loves his neighbor has fulfilled the law. For this, 'YOU SHALL NOT COMMIT ADULTERY, YOU SHALL NOT MURDER, YOU SHALL NOT STEAL, YOU SHALL NOT COVET, and if there is any other commandment, it is summed up in this saying, 'YOU SHALL LOVE YOUR NEIGHBOR AS YOURSELF.' Love does no wrong to a neighbor; therefore love is the fulfillment of the law." (Romans 13:8-10) Here Paul quoted four of the Ten Commandments. Plus, He quoted the second great commandment affirmed by Jesus. Clearly both Jesus and

Paul kept the Ten Commandments. I quoted other New Testament writers earlier in this book to show that they likewise observed the Ten Commandments.

At an absolute minimum, then, the New Testament writers observed the two most important commandments declared by Jesus and the Ten Commandments declared verbally by the LORD at Mt. Sinai. These were the commandments which they emphasized the most. Moreover, these were the commandments which they used as examples of loving behavior. As noted earlier in this book, the New Testament writers emphasized love. And loving behavior they repeatedly associated with keeping the two most important commandments and the Ten Commandments.

The New Testament writers frequently quoted Old Testament commandments. For example, when Jesus declared the two most important commandments in the law in Matthew 22:37-40, He was quoting from Deuteronomy 6:5 and Leviticus 19:18. Similarly, when Jesus overcame the temptations of the devil in Matthew 4:1-11, three times He quoted from the Old Testament. Matthew 4:4 is a quote of the last part of Deuteronomy 8:3, Matthew 4:7 is a quote of Deuteronomy 6:16, and Matthew 4:10 is a quote of Deuteronomy 6:13. Since Jesus quoted these commandments to overcome the devil, I am sure that the New Testament writers believed that they were still in force. Likewise, Jesus declared, "It is written, 'AND MY HOUSE SHALL BE A HOUSE OF PRAYER.'" (Luke 19:46) This is a quote from Isaiah 56:7. I still believe that God's house is a house of prayer. I am sure that the New Testament writers believed likewise.

Jesus also expanded some commandments from the Old Testament. "You have heard that the ancients were told, 'YOU SHALL NOT COMMIT MURDER' and 'Whoever commits murder shall be liable to the court.' But I say to you that everyone who is angry with his brother shall be guilty before the court; and whoever says to his brother, 'You good-for-nothing,' shall be guilty before the supreme court; and whoever says, 'You fool,' shall be guilty enough to go into the fiery hell." (Matthew 5:21-22) The sixth commandment instructs us not to murder. But Jesus commanded us not to even get angry at our brother. We are still not supposed to murder, but now we are not even supposed to get angry at our brother.

Likewise, Jesus declared: "You have heard that it was said, 'YOU SHALL NOT COMMIT ADULTERY'; but I say to you that everyone who looks at a woman with lust for her has already committed adultery with her in his heart." (Matthew 5:27-28) The seventh commandment instructs us not to commit adultery. But Jesus commanded us not to even look on a woman with lust. We are still not supposed to commit adultery, but now we are not even supposed to look on a woman with lust.

Jesus stated very plainly: "if you love Me, you will keep My commandments." (John 14:15) His commandments include both His updates to Old Testament commandments and new commandments which He gave. Here are four of Jesus' new commandments in just one verse: "But I say unto you, Love your enemies, bless them that curse you, do good to them that hate you, and pray for them which despitefully use you, and persecute you." (Matthew 5:44 KJV) There are no Old Testament commandments to love your enemies, bless those who curse you, do good to those who hate you, and pray for your persecutors. But I am confident that the New Testament writers endeavored to keep these commandments given by Jesus Himself.

In regard to commandments, the apostle Peter made this statement: "This second epistle, beloved, I now write unto you; in both which I stir up your pure minds by way of remembrance: that ye may be mindful of the words which were spoken before by the holy prophets, and of the commandments of us the apostles of the Lord and Savior." (II Peter 3:1-2 KJV) According to the apostle Peter's own words, we are to obey "the words" of "the holy prophets" and "the commandments" of "the apostles." Yes, we are to obey the commandments of Jesus, but we are also to obey the commandments of His holy apostles.

In I Thessalonians 5:16-18 we find three apostolic commandments. The apostle Paul commanded us as follows: "Rejoice always; pray without ceasing; in everything give thanks; for this is God's will for you in Christ Jesus." There are commandments to rejoice in the Old Testament, but I don't recall an Old Testament commandment to "rejoice always." There are commandments to pray in the Old Testament, but I don't recall an Old Testament commandment to "pray without ceasing." There are commandments to give thanks in the Old Testament, but I don't recall an Old Testament commandment to "give thanks" "in everything." I believe that the writers of the New Testament kept their own apostolic commandments and taught their disciples to do likewise. Moreover, I believe that we do well today when we "rejoice always," "pray without ceasing," and "give thanks" "in everything."

What about Old Testament commandments not included in the Ten Commandments, not reinforced by Jesus or the apostles, and not included in the commandments of Jesus or the apostles? Did the New Testament writers keep these other commandments? I don't know. What I do know is that if they did, they did not emphasize them as much as the commandments covered in this chapter. We would do well to do likewise. Let's emphasize the commandments we find in the New Testament – not the ones we don't.

CHAPTER 20

PUTTING IT ALL TOGETHER

As I stated at the beginning of this book, I want the faith once delivered to the saints. As I established throughout this book, the faith once delivered to the saints is the faith of 1st Century Christianity. However, in chapters 16 and 17 of this book, I demonstrated that the modern Bible-believing Christian church emphasizes most of the truths emphasized by the writers of the New Testament. We want to keep emphasizing those truths while reestablishing all the truths which the 1st Century church maintained.

Although modern Sabbath keepers have restored the seventh-day Sabbath observed by the 1st Century church, many of them have tended to neglect to emphasize the main truths that the 1st Century church emphasized. I went through those truths in chapters 16 and 17. But they are so important that I will go through them again. The New Testament church emphasized Jesus – Jesus as Savior, Jesus as Christ, and Jesus as Lord. They emphasized that salvation is through Jesus Christ and no one else. Plus, they declared over and over again that salvation is in the person of Jesus Christ and not in any list of dos and don'ts.

The New Testament writers put major emphasis on the death, burial, and resurrection of Jesus Christ. They clearly taught that Christians should identify with Christ in His death, burial, and resurrection. Look at any message that Peter or Paul gave in Acts and you will see the emphasis on the death, burial, and resurrection of Jesus Christ.

The New Testament writers emphasized grace and faith. Although they still observed the commandments of God, they knew that they were not saved by keeping the commandments of God. They were saved by grace through faith without any works of the law. We want to retain this emphasis while also recovering their emphasis on the commandments of God.

"For this is the love of God, that we keep His commandments; and His commandments are not burdensome." (I John 5:3) In this Scripture the apostle John defines the love of God as keeping the commandments of God. We Christians all say that we love God, but to prove that we do we need to keep His commandments. As I stated previously in this book, at the minimum this means that we observe the Ten Commandments. Do we get saved by keeping the Ten Commandments? No. Do we stay saved by keeping the Ten Commandments? No. Do we show God that we love Him by keeping the Ten Commandments? Yes.

Why am I going over this again? Many modern Sabbath keepers state that they are saved by grace, but then turn around and declare that they continue to be saved by keeping the Ten Commandments. This is error pure and simple. Paul wrote the book of Galatians specifically to deal with this error. "You have been severed from Christ, you who are seeking to be justified by the law; you have fallen from grace." (Galatians 5:4) I have never seen a modern Sabbath keeper (other than myself) deal with this verse. Our theology is only correct if we deal with all the Scriptures on a subject – and particularly all the Scriptures in the New Testament on that subject.

"For what the law could not do, weak as it was through the flesh, God did: sending His own Son in the likeness of sinful flesh and as an offering for sin, He condemned sin in the flesh, so that the requirement of the Law might be fulfilled in us, who do not walk according to the flesh, but according to the Spirit." (Romans 8:3-4) Many Christians like to quote Romans 8:3 while neglecting Romans 8:4. Can we get the victory over sin though keeping the law? No. Romans 8:3 and many other verses tell us that we cannot get the victory over sin through keeping the law. But Romans 8:4 teaches us that the requirement of the law is fulfilled in us when we walk according to the Spirit. What is the requirement of the law? The requirement of the law is that we keep God's commandments. Romans 8:4 teaches us that we need to walk according to the Holy Spirit to keep God's commandments.

"For this is the love of God, that we keep His commandments; and HIS COMMANDMENTS ARE NOT BURDENSOME." (I John 5:3 – Emphasis mine) I quoted this verse above; now I quote it again with the emphasis on the last phrase. Often Christians say, "I don't want to get hung up on dos and don'ts" or "I don't want be overburdened by rules and regulations." What are they really saying? Thay are saying that God's commandments are burdensome in direct opposition to God's Word. We will never return to the emphasis of the New Testament writers until we change our attitude about the commandments of God.

All of this brings us back to the fourth commandment – that is, the Sabbath commandment. Most of the Christian church teaches that the Sabbath has been changed to Sunday. We went through the whole matter of the Sabbath in chapters 12 and 13 of this book. There we showed that all the New Testament writers continued to observe the seventh-day Sabbath and taught their disciples to likewise observe the seventh-day Sabbath. They taught their disciples to attend synagogue services and synagogue services were on the Sabbath.

Did the New Testament writers emphasize the Sabbath to the degree that many modern Sabbath keepers do today? No, they did not. But they kept the Sabbath and they taught their disciples to keep the Sabbath. The change from Biblical Sabbath-keeping to Roman Sunday-keeping did not occur until early in the 2nd Century in the Western churches of the Roman Empire. The Eastern churches of the Roman Empire continued to observe the seventh-day Sabbath until at least the 4th Century. To this day the Roman Catholic Church declares that they changed the weekly holy day from Sabbath to Sunday. In fact, they affirm authority over most Protestant churches because most Protestant churches have followed them in changing the Biblical Sabbath to the Roman Sunday. If you want to know more on this subject, I strongly recommend the book *From Sabbath to Sunday* included in the bibliography.

The New Testament writers also emphasized love, the leading of the Holy Spirit, and the second coming of Jesus Christ. The modern Bible-believing Christian church has done likewise with love and the second coming of Jesus Christ. As a whole, the modern Bible-believing Christian church has taught love more than they have walked in love. Again, if we do better at loving God through keeping His commandments, we will do better at loving one another.

How important is the leading of the Holy Spirit? The apostles who wrote the New Testament didn't do anything without the leading of the Holy Spirit. The apostle Paul wrote: "For all who are being led by the Spirit of God, these are sons of God." (Romans 8:14) In the 1st Century Christian church, to be considered a son of God, you needed to learn to be led by the Spirit of God. I will take up the matter of the leading of the Holy Spirit more fully in the next chapter.

In this book, I also addressed the matter of how the New Testament writers kept track of time. They all kept track of time according to the Biblical calendar, using the Biblical day, the Biblical week, the Biblical month, and the Biblical year. None of them used the Roman time concepts which we use today. We will do better at getting our modern Christianity in line with New Testament Christianity if we make the effort to change our thinking about time. For example, as I am adding this paragraph to this chapter today, it is New Year's Day January 1st, 2024, on the Roman calendar. But it is not New Year's Day on God's Biblical calendar. On God's Biblical calendar it is the 20th day of the tenth month. New Year's Day on God's Biblical calendar generally occurs in March or early April on the Roman calendar.

In the context of God's Biblical calendar, I took up the Biblical feasts. Jesus Christ died on the day of Passover on God's calendar and was resurrected from the grave during the Feast of Unleavened Bread on God's calendar. He poured out the Holy Spirit on the day of Pentecost on God's calendar. God does important things on days on His calendar – not on days on the manmade

Roman calendar. In the future He will continue to do important things on days on His calendar and particularly on days of the fall feasts.

I also addressed the New Testament writers' view of Israel. Although most of the 1st Century Jews rejected the gospel of Jesus Christ, Paul made clear in Romans 11 that God still has a plan for Israel. In spite of the fact that most Jews continue to reject the gospel, in the end all Israel will be saved. (Romans 11:26) If some 1st Century Jews had not received Jesus Christ as their Lord and Savior and then preached the gospel to us Gentiles, we would still be in our sins. As noted in the very first chapter of this book, all the New Testament writers were either Jews or converted Jews. And they all had a Jewish worldview.

Finally, I took up the matter of the name of Yeshua. This is the name which was used by the 1st Century Christian church to refer to the Son of God. Our Lord wasn't called Jesus then; the English language hadn't even been invented in the 1st Century A.D. We now know that Yeshua is an accurate English transliteration of the original Aramaic name of the Son of God. Why do we then continue to use Jesus, which is a much less accurate transliteration?

CHAPTER 21

WHERE DO WE GO FROM HERE?

One thing that we cannot do from here is go back to the Jewish synagogue. The unbelieving Jews of the 1st Century put the believing Jews out of the synagogue. So we cannot go back to the Jewish synagogue as the 1st Century Christians did. Of course, we can visit synagogue services to understand modern Judaism better. But until the Jews accept Yeshua as their Messiah, the synagogue cannot be the place of Christian worship.

What was the experience and belief of the New Testament writers in regard to the Holy Spirit? Matthew, Peter, and John were all present on the Day of Pentecost; so they all received the baptism in the Holy Spirit with speaking in tongues. (See Acts 1:13 and Acts 2:1-4.) James (who wrote the Epistle of James) was also present on the Day of Pentecost; so he likewise received the baptism in the Holy Spirit with speaking in tongues. (See Acts 1:13-14 and Acts 2:1-4.) Mark was a disciple of Peter. Since Peter firmly believed that the baptism in the Holy Spirit was an important experience for Christians (see Acts 2:16-18 and Acts 11:15-17), certainly he made sure that Mark received the baptism in the Holy Spirit. Paul received the baptism in the Holy Spirit (Acts 9:17) and spoke in tongues (I Corinthians 14:18). That leaves just Luke and Jude. Luke was a disciple of Paul. Would not Paul have made sure that Luke received the baptism in the Holy Spirit? Moreover, Luke recorded five accounts of Christians receiving the baptism in the Holy Spirit in Acts. I do not believe that Luke would have recorded all these accounts if he himself had not been baptized in the Holy Spirit. We don't know about Jude, but since all the other writers of the New Testament received the baptism in the Holy Spirit, it is reasonable to believe that Jude had this experience as well.

Now I am with the writers of New Testament on the baptism in the Holy Spirit. So I am also with modern Pentecostals and Charismatics on this matter. I believe that there are two distinct experiences in the Holy Spirit – one when you receive Jesus as your Lord and Savior and another when you receive the baptism in the Holy Spirit.

Both the Pentecostal and the Charismatic movements started with great manifestations of the power of God. In the Pentecostal movement, the outpouring of the Holy Spirit occurred between 1900 and 1910. Again there was a brief outpouring of the Holy Spirit among Pentecostals in the Latter Rain movement of 1948 and 1949. In the Charismatic movement, the outpouring of the Holy Spirit occurred between 1964 and 1973. Nothing like these outpourings of the Holy Spirit has happened since.

In the beginning of both the Pentecostal and the Charismatic movements, there were great manifestations of the Holy Spirit. Believers didn't just speak in tongues. They prophesied, they healed the sick, and they cast out demons. In fact, they manifested all nine gifts of the Holy Spirit. (See I Corinthians 12:7-11.) The apostle Paul wrote: "But to each one is given the manifestation of the spirit for the common good." (I Corinthians 12:7) The gifts of the Holy Spirit are given "to each one" in the body of Christ. The gifts aren't just for spiritual superstars; they are for every member of the body of Christ. At the start of the Charismatic movement, many believers manifested the gifts of the Holy Spirit. Today very few believers in either the Pentecostal or the Charismatic movement manifest the gifts of the Holy Spirit.

What has gone wrong? Why don't we have the complete faith of the New Testament writers today? In Sabbath-keeping groups, the Lord has worked to restore the Sabbath and the commandments to His church, but the Sunday-keeping Bible-believing churches have so far passed on these truths. Instead, they have retained the Roman Sunday over the Christian Sabbath (the Sabbath being from sundown Friday through sundown Saturday). Moreover, most of these Sunday-keeping Bible-believing churches have continued to affirm that the law is done way with when it is clearly not done away with. You can neither get saved nor stay saved by keeping God's commandments, but the New Testament writers clearly taught that the Holy Spirit would lead you to keep the commandments of God.

Every Sunday-keeping, Bible-believing Christian leader I know is looking for another move of God. I have a couple of suggestions. First, start keeping the Sabbath. If you have a job where you work on the Sabbath, get a different job where you don't have to work on the Sabbath. Stop doing work projects at home on the Sabbath. And start meeting with other believers on the Sabbath. In fact, make the Sabbath meeting your primary church meeting. Am I against Sunday meetings? No, but if you don't make the Sabbath meeting your primary church meeting, your tendency will be to do projects at home on the Sabbath. Possibly you could have a period of transition where you meet on both the Sabbath and Sunday. But the sooner you make your Sabbath meeting your primary church meeting, the sooner you will be meeting as the 1st Century Christians did.

In Matthew 22:36 we find a Pharisee asking Jesus this question: "Teacher, which is the great commandment in the Law?" Jesus replied as follows: "And He said to him, 'YOU SHALL LOVE THE LORD YOUR GOD WITH ALL YOUR HEART, AND WITH ALL YOUR SOUL, AND WITH ALL YOUR MIND.' This is the greatest and foremost commandment. The second is like it, 'YOU SHALL LOVE YOUR NEIGHBOR AS YOURSLEF.' On these two commandments depend the whole Law and the Prophets." (Mathew 22:37-40) Now look at the Ten Commandments. The first four have to do with loving God with all your heart, soul, and mind. And the last six have to do with loving your neighbor as yourself.

I will again use the Sabbath as an example. Do I keep the Sabbath to get saved? No. Do I keep the Sabbath to stay saved? No. I keep the Sabbath to show God that I love Him with all my heart, mind, and soul. Many times I have been called a legalist for keeping the Sabbath. But I don't observe the Sabbath for any legalistic reason. I observe the Sabbath because I love God. I observe the Sabbath because "this is the love of God, that we keep His commandments; and His commandments are not burdensome." (I John 5:3)

All the writers of the New Testament were schooled in the law (the first five books of the Bible). They quoted from the law repeatedly and they memorized many Scriptures from the law. Today we would do well to memorize Scriptures from the law other than the ordinances. The book of Deuteronomy reviews the main commandments of the law without reviewing the main ordinances of the law. In fact, Deuteronomy means second law. So my second suggestion is to memorize at least ten Scriptures from the book of Deuteronomy. A list of recommended Scriptures from Deuteronomy is in the Postscript to this book.

Finally, I am looking for a revival. I believe that if Bible-believing Christians get serious about keeping God's commandments and then fast and pray for a revival, a revival will be on the way. The Lord created a powerful move of God among Jesus-preaching, Holy Spirit-filled, commandment-keeping believers in the 1st Century Christian church. I believe that He can do the same for Jesus-preaching, Holy Spirit-filled, commandment-keeping Christians today. "Here is the perseverance of the saints who keep the commandments of God and their faith in Jesus." (Revelation 14:12)

POSTSCRIPT

Near the end of this book, I suggested that you memorize at least 10 verses from Deuteronomy. In this postscript, I list some of the best verses from Deuteronomy. All verses are quoted from the King James Version because it goes verse by verse. However, since the King James Version does not use modern English, I suggest that you memorize at least 10 verses from Deuteronomy from either the New American Standard Version or the New King James Version of the Bible.

Closely related thoughts are given in successive paragraphs with no space between them. So the Scriptures in Deuteronomy 5:6-21 are quoted in successive paragraphs with no space between them because these verses restate the Ten Commandments (first given in Exodus 20:1-17).

5:6 "I am the LORD YOUR God which brought thee out of the land of Egypt, from the house of bondage."
5:7 "Thou shalt have none other gods before me."
5:8 "Thou shalt not make unto thee any graven image, or any likeness of any thing that is in heaven above, or that is in the earth beneath, or that is in the waters beneath the earth."
5:9 "Thou shalt not bow down to them, nor serve them: for I the LORD your God am a jealous God,
visiting the iniquity of the fathers upon the children unto the third and fourth generation of them that hate me,"
5:10 "And shewing mercy unto thousands of them that love me and keep my commandments."

The New Testament Writer's Worldview

5:11 "Thou shalt not take the name of the LORD thy God in vain: for the LORD will not hold him guiltless that taketh his name in vain."

5:12 "Keep the sabbath day to sanctify it, as the LORD thy God hath commanded thee."

5:13 "Six days thou shalt labour, and do all thy work:"

5:14 "But the seventh day is the sabbath of the LORD thy God: in it thou shalt not do any work, thou, nor thy son, nor thy daughter, nor thy manservant, nor thy maidservant, nor thine ox, nor thine ass, nor any of thy cattle, nor the stranger that is within thy gates; that thy manservant and thy maidservant may rest as well as thou."

5:15 "And remember that thou wast a servant in the land of Egypt, and that the LORD thy God brought thee out thence through a mighty hand and by a stretched out arm: therefore the LORD thy God commanded thee to keep the sabbath day."

5:16 "Honour thy father and thy mother, as the LORD thy God commanded thee; that thy days may be prolonged , and that it may go well with thee, in the land which the LORD thy God giveth thee."

5:17 "Thou shalt not kill."

5:18 "Neither shalt thou commit adultery."

5:19 "Neither shalt thus steal."

5:20 "Neither shalt thou bear false witness against thy neighbor."

5:21 "Neither shalt thou desire thy neighbour's wife, neither shalt thou covet thy neighbor's house, his field, or his manservant, or his maidservant, his ox, or his ass, or any thing that is thy neighbour's."

6:4 "Hear, O Israel: the LORD our God is one LORD:"

6:5 "And thou shalt love the LORD thy God with all thine heart, and with all thy soul, and with all thy might."

6:6 "And these words, which I command thee this day, shall be in thine heart:"

6:7 "And thou shalt teach them diligently unto thy children, and shalt talk of them when thou sittest in thine house, and when thou walkest by the way, and when thou liest down, and when risest up."

6:8 "And thou shalt bind them for a sign upon thine hand, and they shall be as frontlets between thine eyes."

6:9 "And thou shalt write them upon the posts of thy house, and on thy gates."

10:12 "And now, Israel, what doth the LORD thy God require of thee, but to fear the LORD thy God, to walk in all his ways, and to love him, and to serve the LORD thy God with all thy heart and with all thy soul,"

10:13 "To keep the commandments of the LORD, and his statutes, which I command thee this day for thy good?"

10:14 "Behold, the heaven and the heaven of heavens is the LORD's thy God, the earth also, with all that therein is."

10:15 "Only the LORD had a delight in thy fathers to love them, and he chose their seed after them, even you above all people, as it is this day."

10:16 "Circumcise therefore the foreskin of your heart, and be no more stiffnecked."

10:17 "For the LORD your God is God of gods, and Lord of lords, a great God, a mighty, and a terrible, which regardeth not persons, nor taketh reward:"

10:18 "He doth execute the judgment of the fatherless and widow, and loveth the stranger, in giving him food and raiment."

10:19 "Love ye therefore the stranger: for ye were strangers in the land of Egypt."

12:8 "Ye shall not do after all the things that we do here this day, every man whatsoever is right in his own eyes."

15:7 "If there be among you a poor man of one of thy brethren within any of thy gates in the land which the LORD thy God giveth thee, thou shalt not harden thine heart, nor shut thine hand from thy poor brother:"

15:8 "But thou shalt open thine hand wide unto him, and shalt surely lend him sufficient for his need, in that which he wanteth."

18:9 "When thou art come into the land which the LORD thy God giveth thee, thou shalt not learn to do after the abominations of those nations."

18:10 "There shall not be found among you any one that maketh his son or his daughter to pass through the fire, or that useth divination, or an observer of times, or an enchanter, or a witch,"

18:11 "Or a charmer, or a consulter with familiar spirits, or a wizard, or a necromancer."

18:12 "For all that do these things are an abomination unto the LORD: and because of these abominations the LORD thy God doth drive them out from before thee."

18:18 "I will raise up a Prophet from among their brethren, like unto thee, and will put my words in his mouth; and he shall speak unto them all that I shall command him."

18:19 "And It shall come to pass, that whosoever will not hearken unto my words which he shall speak in my name, I will require it of him."

19:15 "One witness shall not rise up against a man for any iniquity, or for any sin, in any sin that he sinneth: at the mouth of two witnesses, or at the mouth of three witnesses, shall the matter be established."

22:5 "The woman shall not wear that which pertaineth unto a man, neither shall a man put on a woman's garment: for all that do so are abomination unto the LORD thy God."

24:17 "Thou shalt not pervert the judgment of the stranger, nor of the fatherless, nor take a widow's raiment to pledge:"
24:18 "But thou shalt remember that thou wast a bondman in Egypt, and the LORD thy God redeemed thee thence: therefore I command thee to do this thing."
24:19 "When thou cuttest down thine harvest in thy field, and hast forgot a sheaf in the field, thou shalt not go again to fetch it: it shall be for the stranger, for the fatherless, and for the widow: that the LORD thy God may bless thee in all the work of thine hands."

In closing, I comment on just two of these passages from Deuteronomy. Deuteronomy 18:18-19 is a prediction of the ultimate prophet Jesus Christ. As Christians, we believe that Jesus Christ fulfilled the prophecy given through Moses in Deuteronomy 18:18-19.

Deuteronomy 19:15 gives one of the main principles on which our legal system is based. To this day we require the word of two or three witnesses to convict a criminal. No one is to be convicted on the word of just one witness.

Now read back over the verses quoted from Deuteronomy and think about how they still apply to our lives as Christians today. The fact that these verses still apply to our lives today means that the law is not done away with.

BIBLIOGRAPHY

I have been reading books and articles on the 1st Century Christian church for over 50 years of my life. I do not recall all the books and articles that I have read on this subject. So some of the works that have contributed to my thinking about the worldview of the New Testament writers are not included in this bibliography. This is not intentional on my part; I have simply forgotten some of the works which I have read on this subject.

There is one article listed in the bibliography which I just scanned rather than read: "Are the Ten Commandments Upheld in the New Testament?" From scanning this article, I could tell that the author's view regarding the Ten Commandments is close to mine. All the other books and articles listed in the bibliography I have read in their entirety.

The primary source for this book is the Holy Bible. For the most part, I used the New American Standard Version of the Holy Bible. Occasionally I used the King James Version. Plus, just once I used the New International Version. These three versions of The Holy Bible are noted first:

The Holy Bible: The New American Standard Bible, Copyright 2003 by The Lockman Foundation, Published by Foundation Publications, Inc., La Habra, California.

The Holy Bible: Authorized King James Version, Copyright 2019 by Holman Bible Publishers,

Nashville, Tennessee.

The Holy Bible: The New International Version, Copyright 1973, 1978, 1984, 2011 by Biblica, Inc., 1820 Jet Stream Drive, Colorado Springs, CO 80921.

Other works which have contributed to my thinking regarding the worldview of the New Testament writers are as follows:

Plato's Shadow: The Hellenizing of Christianity, written by Gary Petty, Copyright 2013 by Gary Petty, Published by Little Frog Publishing, Round Rock, Texas.

From Sabbath to Sunday, Written by Samuele Bacchiocchi, Copyright 1975 & 2005 by Samuele Bacchiocchi, Republished by Biblical Perspectives, 4990 Appian Way, Berrien Springs, Michigan with permission from the original publisher The Pontifical Gregorian University Press, Rome, Italy, 1977.

History of the Sabbath, Written by J. N. Andrews, First Published by Review & Herald Publishing Association, Battle Creek, Michigan and Pacific Press, Oakland, California, 1887, Copyright 1998 by TEACH Services, Inc. Republished by TEACH Services, Inc., 140 Industry Ln SW, Calhoun, Georgia.

The Sabbaths of God, Written by James L. Porter, Copyright 1966 by James L. Porter, Published by Exposition Press Inc., 386 Park Ave. So., New York, New York.

The Apostolic Constitutions, authors unknown, likely written in the 2nd and 3rd Centuries A.D. and compiled in the 4th Century A.D., republished by many different publishers.

"The Ancient Synagogue in Israel & the Diaspora", Written by Dana Murray, Published in the World History Encyclopedia, 2015.

"What the Bible Says about Proselytes", Article Published in the Berean: Daily Verse and Comment, Copyright 1992-2023 by Church of the Great God, 10409 Barberville Rd., Fort Mill, South Carolina.

"God-fearer", Article Published in Wikipedia, 2023.

"Are the Ten Commandments Upheld in the New Testament?", Written by David Treybig, Article Published in Life, Hope, and Truth, Publication of the Church of God, a Worldwide Association, Inc., P O Box 3490, McKinney, Texas.

Online Etymology Dictionary, entry for "Jesus". The *Online Etymology Dictionary* lists as its primary sources *An Etymological Dictionary of Modern English* and *A Comprehensive Etymological Dictionary of the English Language.*

www.ingramcontent.com/pod-product-compliance
Lightning Source LLC
Chambersburg PA
CBHW052145070526
44585CB00017B/1984